BEST-LOVED
Recipes

Publications International, Ltd.

Special thanks to the Campbell's Kitchen, Lucinda Ayers, Vice President, and Catherine Marschean-Spivak, Group Manager.

Photography on pages 55, 58, 63, 66, 68, 70, 71, 73, 94, 119, 124, 159, 189, 193, 199, 202, 203, 211, 214, 221, 223, 226 and 231 by Stephen Hamilton Photographics, Inc., Chicago.

Pictured on the front cover: Tuna Noodle Casserole *(page 189).*

Pictured on the back cover (clockwise from top): Green Bean Casserole *(page 218)*, Sausage, Beef & Bean Casserole *(page 203)*, Spiced Tomato Soup Cancakes *(page 248)* and Chicken & Roasted Garlic Risotto *(page 100)*.

ISBN-13: 978-1-60553-467-1
ISBN-10: 1-60553-467-6
Library of Congress: 2009938813

Manufactured in China.

8 7 6 5 4 3 2 1

Microwave Cooking: Microwave ovens vary in wattage. Use the cooking times as guidelines and check for doneness before adding more time.

Preparation/Cooking Times: Preparation times are based on the approximate amount of time required to assemble the recipe before cooking, baking, chilling or serving. These times include preparation steps such as measuring, chopping and mixing. The fact that some preparations and cooking can be done simultaneously is taken into account. Preparation of optional ingredients and serving suggestions is not included.

Contents

Getting Started

We in Campbell's Kitchen are so proud to bring you our newest cookbook, *Best-Loved Recipes*. Most cooks, whether experienced or just getting started in the kitchen, have one essential cookbook; the book they turn to whenever they have a question about an unfamiliar ingredient or technique, the one they open when they want to learn how to prepare a new kind of dish. We're hoping this cookbook will become that book for you.

So we've packed it, not just with our favorite recipes, old and new, but also with useful information about all aspects of cooking and the kitchen. We want this to be the book you turn to when you need cooking information, when you need to know the difference between braise and broil, chop and dice or an herb and a spice. We want you to pick up *Best-Loved Recipes* when you need to know how much food to serve at a party, how to make an

ingredient substitution or where to find the definition of a cooking term. So we have provided over 30 pages of cooking advice, glossaries and recommendations, plus charts about herbs and spices, food safety information and everything from tips on buying cookware to how to stock your pantry.

Since 1940, Campbell's Kitchen has been proud to help feed America's families, not just by creating delicious soups, broths and other foods, but also by offering ways to use those foods in family-pleasing recipes that over the years have become part of our culture and our cuisine. Now we hope *Best-Loved Recipes* will become an essential part of your kitchen, becoming well-worn and well-thumbed, favorite recipe pages stained with splashes of Tomato Soup, marked with reminders of special touches you added to a recipe the last time you served it and always at the ready to answer your questions and offer you inspiration for your next delicious meal.

MEASURING UP

Measuring ingredients accurately and correctly is an important part of following a recipe. Using the wrong tools or using the right ones incorrectly can lead to disasters in the kitchen. Here are a few tips:

Measuring Liquid Ingredients

We're all familiar with measuring cups for liquids: They have a pour spout and markings on the outside. Most are glass, although there are plastic ones, too. Most cooks don't differentiate between measuring cups for dry ingredients and liquids, but the truth is, you can't get an accurate measurement if you use the wrong measuring cup. To measure liquid accurately, place the cup on a level work surface. Fill to the desired mark, then bend down to check the measurement at eye level. (If you pick up the cup and hold it to your eyes, you might not hold it level, and you could get an inaccurate measurement.)

A new measuring cup on the market doesn't require stooping: It lets you check the measurement by looking down into the cup rather than stooping to see the mark at eye level. Measures are written on the inside of the cup rather than on the outside.

Liquid measuring cups come in several sizes, and which ones you should have in your kitchen is purely up to you. A 1- or 2-cup measure is a basic necessity. A larger one is also a good idea: A 2-quart glass measure is not only a great mixing bowl, but it also comes in handy when measuring large amounts of liquids for soup or pasta.

Measuring Dry Ingredients

Dry measuring cups are the ones without spouts. They are usually metal or plastic and come nested together. They generally come in ¼-cup, ⅓-cup, ½-cup and 1-cup sizes, although some sets also include a ⅔-cup and a ¾-cup measure. To measure accurately, fill the measure to overflowing with a spoon and with the straight edge of a knife or a metal spatula, sweep across the top of the cup to level the ingredient. Don't dip a measuring cup into flour or other dry ingredients; this compacts the ingredient and will result in an inaccurate measure.

Measuring spoons are used for both dry and wet ingredients. A set of measuring spoons generally includes ¼ teaspoon, ½ teaspoon,

Common Abbreviations

t. or tsp. = teaspoon
T. or Tbsp. = tablespoon
c. = cup
oz. = ounce
pt. = pint
qt. = quart
gal. = gallon
lb. = pound

Basic Measures

1 tablespoon = 3 teaspoons
2 tablespoons = 1 fluid ounce
1 cup = 16 tablespoons
1 cup = 8 fluid ounces
1 pint = 2 cups
1 pint = 16 fluid ounces
1 quart = 4 cups (2 pints)
1 quart = 32 fluid ounces
1 gallon = 16 cups (8 pints
or 4 quarts)

1 teaspoon and 1 tablespoon. Some sets include ⅛ teaspoon and 1½ teaspoons. When measuring dry ingredients, do the same as you do with the measuring cups: Fill the spoon to overflowing, then level it off with a knife or a metal spatula. Measure liquid ingredients by filling the spoon to the rim.

And one more thing: Always measure an ingredient over a bowl or piece of waxed paper, so that if it overflows it has someplace to go other than in your recipe!

COMMON KITCHEN TOOLS

Blender: An electric appliance that blends liquid and soft food mixtures and can also be used for small chopping jobs. If you don't own a blender, you can use a food processor fitted with a steel blade for blending. The new handheld immersion blenders can be placed directly into a bowl or pot of food; they come in handy as transferring hot food out of the pot and into an appliance can be dangerous. *See Food Processor.*

Box Grater: Used to shred and grate foods. Most box graters are

made of metal and have a handle on top. There are sharp holes of varying sizes on all sides of the grater; most also have a slot suitable for slicing foods such as cucumbers or carrots.

Can Opener: Can openers come in two basic varieties—manual and electric—and can cost from a dollar or two on up. There are a couple of types of manual ones: Some are handheld, others attach to the wall or cabinet. Some cut the lid just inside the rim of the can; others cut off the lid around the sides of the can. Electric can openers are available in several varieties: cordless, under-counter, countertop and even portable. Some have knife sharpeners, bottle openers, an automatic shutoff and detachable arms that are dishwasher-safe. Look for a model that can open cans of any size.

Colander: Used to strain or drain liquids from foods, such as water from cooked pasta. Make sure the colander you're using has holes that are smaller than the food you're draining.

Food Processor: This handy machine has a blade that can be used for anything from coarse chopping to puréeing. Plus, its attachments make shredding, slicing, mixing and kneading a snap. *See Blender.*

Kitchen or Poultry Shears: Used to perform cutting tasks that are more easily done with a scissors than with a knife, such as cutting up pieces of chicken. Keep kitchen shears for kitchen tasks only; using them to cut poster board for the kids or opening cardboard boxes will quickly dull the blades.

Knives: High-quality knives are a good investment because, if you take care of them, they will last a lifetime. Look for high-carbon steel knives that extend through the handle (called the tang) for good balance and longer life. The chef's knife is the kitchen workhorse, because it can be used to chop, slice, dice and mince. Also useful are: a paring knife for small cutting and peeling jobs, a serrated knife for bread, tomatoes and other tough-skinned foods and a boning and slicing knife for meat. Buy a butcher's steel, and keep knives well sharpened. Wash knives by hand with warm soapy water, and dry immediately and thoroughly so they won't rust.

Mixers: A hand-held mixer can accomplish all but the most difficult mixing jobs, and is used anytime a recipe calls for an electric mixer. Stand mixers are more powerful and can handle the toughest mixing jobs, including kneading bread dough; they also have the added benefit of being hands-free and easier on the cook.

Pepper Mill: Essential for recipes calling for freshly ground black pepper. Some have a grinding mechanism that can be adjusted for fine or coarse grinds.

Spatulas: Also called scrapers or rubber scrapers, spatulas are made from rubber or heat-resistant silicone with wood or plastic handles. These handy tools are invaluable for many scraping, mixing and stirring tasks. They come in various sizes (small to large) and shapes (flat and curved). We recommend keeping a few different sizes handy.

Spoons: Used for mixing, stirring and serving. Slotted spoons are useful for removing solid foods from their cooking liquid. Wooden spoons stay cool to the touch and are sturdy enough to mix dense cookie dough or thick batter. (Always use wood or plastic spoons and utensils with nonstick cookware; metal ones will scratch the nonstick coating, which could then flake off into food.)

Tongs: Used to grab food when a fork or spoon can't quite do the job—for example, to turn pieces of chicken in a skillet or to remove whole green beans from a pan. Tongs can be made of plastic, metal or wood; some feature a spring-loaded handle or a sliding ring that locks the tongs to the grasp you need.

Vegetable Peeler: Used to remove the peel or skin of vegetables, such as potatoes, carrots and cucumbers. Peelers can also be used to shave hard cheeses, such as Parmesan, to remove zest from lemons, limes and oranges and to make curls from chocolate.

Whisk: A stirring tool made of metal or plastic that's invaluable for beating eggs, whipping cream or making mayonnaise, salad dressings or other sauces. Use a whisk any time you're making a batter or sauce that must be free of lumps, or when you're emulsifying an oil-based mixture such as a salad dressing. Also called a whip.

COMMON COOKING TERMS

Al dente: Describes cooked pasta that is still a little firm. In Italian, it means "to the tooth".

Bake: To cook food by dry heat, usually in an oven, convection oven, toaster oven or even a slow cooker for some recipes.

Baste: To brush or spoon liquid or melted fat over food during cooking. Basting keeps food moist as it cooks and adds flavor. Bulb basters are usually used for oven-roasted foods or whole chicken or turkey because they can carry the basting liquid to the dish without dripping.

Batter: The uncooked, liquid mixture for pancakes, cakes, muffins, cupcakes, etc. Batter usually consists of a liquid, such as milk or oil, a dry ingredient, such as flour and sometimes eggs.

Blend: To combine two or more ingredients with a spoon, food processor, blender or whisk, into one uniform mixture.

Boil: To bring a food or a liquid up to bubbling. Technically, to be boiling, bubbles must continuously rise and break at the surface of the food or liquid and continue to do so, even when the food is being stirred. *See Simmer.*

Braising: To cook food (usually meat) on the stovetop, covered, in a little liquid and at a low temperature. Braising is better than roasting for less tender cuts of meat. Try it with short ribs or lamb shanks.

Broil: To cook food directly under a dry heat source, such as an oven broiler or toaster oven broiler. Broiling is great for most steaks and chops, and a broiler can melt a cheese topping on a casserole in just a minute or two.

Brown: To cook food in a little oil or fat until it turns brown. Recipes also may indicate to cook until "golden brown" or "light brown," but to brown a food means to cook,  usually over medium or high heat, and quickly, just until it turns brown.

Chill: To put food in the refrigerator until it's cold. The recipe will usually indicate how long this will take for a particular dish. *See Refrigerate.*

Chop: To cut food into irregularly shaped, bite-size pieces (or smaller) with a  knife or a food processor. Chopped food is larger and more uneven than food that is diced, smaller than food that is cut up and larger than food that is minced. *See Cut up, Dice and Mince.*

Coat: To cover food evenly with a dry ingredient, such as flour or bread crumbs, or with a wet ingredient, such as a batter. An easy way to coat food with dry ingredients is to put them in a plastic or paper bag, add the food, seal and shake; or place them in a soup bowl and gently press the food into the bowl to coat. Foods are usually dipped in beaten egg before coated with dry ingredients, and sometimes they are dipped in flour or cornmeal before they're dipped in batter.

Cool: To let hot food stand at room temperature until it reaches a specific temperature or cools completely. The recipe will usually indicate how long this will take for a particular dish.

Cover: To put a lid, wrap or foil onto or over a container of food. Covering food while it cooks prevents liquids from cooking away, helps the food cook more thoroughly and brings up the temperature inside the pan more quickly.

Crush: To smash food into smaller pieces. Graham and soda crackers, garlic and herbs are often crushed. Dried herbs are easily crushed with your fingers, but an easy way to crush most foods is to put the food in a plastic bag and crush or hit it with your hand, the flat side of a knife or a meat mallet. Or, roll or hit it with a rolling pin. Garlic is usually easily smashed with the flat side of a knife against a wood cutting board.

Cube: To cut food into equal-size cubes about ½-inch in size. Meat and cheese are often cubed.

Cut up: To use a knife or kitchen shears to cut food into smaller pieces that are not necessarily even. This is different from chopping in that the pieces are usually larger than bite-size and are more coarsely cut. *See Chop, Dice and Mince.*

Dice: To cut food into even ¼-inch pieces. *See Cut up, Chop and Mince.*

Dip: To put a food completely into a liquid mixture to coat it. Many foods are dipped into beaten egg, for example, before they are coated. Some fish is dipped into batter before being deep-fried.

Drain: To remove the liquid from a food, usually by pouring the food and the liquid into a colander or a strainer. *See Strain.*

Drizzle: To pour a thin stream of a liquid ingredient, like a sauce over food, such as hot sauce over ice cream. A drizzle does not

completely cover the food.

Fold: To add a food ingredient to a mixture by carefully and lightly mixing it in so that the mixture does not deflate. Usually, a rubber spatula is used, and the food is mixed together in gentle, figure-eight movements.

Garnish: To decorate food with small amounts of other foods. Usually but not always, a garnish is made from food that is already an ingredient in the dish; for example, a basil leaf could garnish a plate of pasta and tomato-basil sauce.

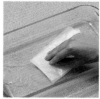

Grate: To mince a food into very small pieces or shreds using a box grater, a food processor or a hand-held grater. Firm foods can be grated more easily than soft foods. Graters usually have several sizes of holes over a rough surface so that foods can be grated to different sizes. *See Shred.*

Grease: To rub a thin layer of oil, shortening, butter or margarine, or to spray nonstick cooking spray on a dish or pan to prevent foods from sticking during cooking or baking.

Greasing also makes cleanup easier. Cooking sprays that combine oil and flour are handy in recipes for baked goods that call for greasing and then flouring pans.

Marinate: To soak or let food stand in a seasoned liquid. The seasoned liquid is called the marinade. Marinating flavors food, and in some cases, it's also done to tenderize food. Usually tenderizing marinades contain some sort of acid, such as lemon juice, vinegar or wine. If you're using a marinade that contains an acid, make sure to use a glass or ceramic dish because acid can react with metal and give the food an off-flavor.

Melt: To use heat to change a solid food into a liquid one, such as heating butter in a saucepan over low heat or melting chocolate in a bowl in the microwave oven.

Microwave: To heat, thaw or cook food in a microwave oven.

Mince: To cut food into very small, irregularly shaped pieces, smaller than chopped or diced. *See Chop, Cut up and Dice.*

Mix: To combine two or more ingredients, usually by stirring with a spoon or a fork or by using an electric mixer, a blender or a food processor.

Peel: To remove the skin of a fruit or a vegetable with a knife, a vegetable peeler or your fingers.

Preheat: To bring heat to the desired temperature before cooking. This usually refers to turning on the oven a few minutes before cooking so that it's at the desired temperature by the time you're ready to cook.

Purée: To turn food into a smooth consistency, usually by using a blender or a food processor. Baby food is a good example of a purée.

Reduce: To cook liquid rapidly, uncovered. Reducing causes the water to evaporate, leaving a thicker and more intensely flavored liquid. It is often called for when making sauces and soups.

Refrigerate: To chill or store food in the refrigerator. These foods usually should be covered to keep them from drying out. *See Chill.*

Roast: To cook meat, poultry, fish, vegetables—even fruit—in an oven. Roasting is mostly done uncovered. Probably more than any other cooking method, roasting brings out the wonderful browned and sweet flavors of foods. Only tender meat cuts should be roasted; other cuts need to be cooked on the stovetop with liquid. *See Braising.*

Roll: To use a rolling pin to flatten dough.

Season: To use pepper, herbs, spices or other seasonings to flavor foods.

Shred: To use the large holes of a grater or food processor to cut food into fine, narrow strips. *See Grate.*

Simmer: To cook liquid gently just below the boiling point. At a simmer, tiny bubbles are just beginning to break the surface of the liquid. *See Boil.*

Slice: To cut food into flat, thin pieces of equal size. The recipe will usually tell you what size to make the slices.

Soften: To set out cold food, such as a stick of butter or package of cream cheese, at room temperature until it softens. You can also soften some foods by zapping them in the microwave for a few seconds on low power. (Be careful; it's easy to melt foods in the microwave before you know it.)

Stew: To cook food slowly in a covered pot. The food is just barely covered in liquid. Stewing usually refers to a mixture of meat, vegetables and liquid and results in fork-tender and flavorful food.

Stir-Fry: To cook food in a small amount of fat, such as oil or butter, over medium-high or high heat, stirring frequently.

Strain: To pour a mixture through a strainer or a piece of cheesecloth. This removes any lumps or chunks of food and provides a clearer liquid. *See Drain.*

Tender-Crisp: To cook food until it is softened but still somewhat crisp to the bite. This usually applies to vegetables. Cooking vegetables until they're tender-crisp retains much of their flavor, nutrients and color.

Toast: To brown food in a toaster, oven or in a skillet.

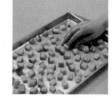

Toss: To mix ingredients gently by using two utensils to lift and drop them in a bowl or other container. Most of the time, tossing refers to mixing ingredients in a salad after the dressing is added.

Zest: The very outer layer of the peel of citrus fruits. To remove the zest, use a sharp paring knife, a vegetable peeler or a special tool called a zester. (Be careful to remove only the colored part and not the white pith, which will give zest a bitter taste.) Zest is quite flavorful and lends a sharp citrus flavor to the dish. Dried zest can be found in the spice aisle of the supermarket.

HERBS AND SPICES

Judging from the popularity of spice stores and the availability of fresh herbs in supermarkets these days, herbs and spices have never been more in demand.

Herbs are the aromatic and flavorful leaves of herbaceous plants (plants with stems that are soft rather than woody). They are available fresh or dried, but can be easily grown in the home garden or on the kitchen windowsill.

Spices are the ground or whole seeds, bark, roots, fruit or flowers of plants. For thousands of years, spices were an important world commodity, actively traded and in part responsible for expeditions that led to the discovery of the New World. During the Middle Ages, the demand for spices in Europe was so great that they were considered as valuable as gold.

Buying Tips

When purchasing fresh herbs, look for brightly colored, fresh-looking leaves without any brown spots or signs of wilting. Even dried herbs and spices can lose their flavor punch, so buy small amounts of those you use infrequently.

Storage

Fresh herbs are perishable, so just buy small amounts at a time. For the short-term, put them in water like flowers; cover leaves loosely with a plastic bag or plastic wrap and store in the refrigerator. If the stems aren't long enough for that, simply wrap them in plastic wrap and keep in the crisper drawer of the fridge. They will last from two days (basil, chives, dill, mint, oregano) to five days (rosemary, sage, tarragon, thyme).

Store your herbs and spices in a cool, dry place in tightly covered containers. Don't store them above the range because the heat and moisture from cooking will cause them to deteriorate more quickly. Mark containers of dried herbs and spices with the purchase date. Leafy herbs and ground spices can remain flavorful for up to 2 to 3 years, whole spices for up to 4 years. Whole peppercorns, nutmeg and cinnamon sticks will keep their flavor for long periods of time, as will potent whole spices like cloves, cumin and cardamom. To check an herb's flavor, crumble a small amount between your fingers and sniff: A strong smell indicates it still has flavoring power.

Spice Blends

Spice blends, available in the spice section of the supermarket, have the advantage of convenience. Some of the more common blends are: bouquet garni, fines herbes, Herbes de Provence, Italian seasoning, poultry seasoning, apple pie spice, celery salt, chili powder, curry powder, five-spice powder, garlic salt, pizza spice, pumpkin pie spice and seasoned salt.

HERBS AND SPICES

HERB OR SPICE	COMMON FORM	CULINARY USE
Allspice (spice)	whole, ground	fruit dishes, stews, pumpkin pie, spicy baked goods
Basil (herb)	fresh, dried, ground	Italian dishes, pesto, salads, soups, stews, tomatoes
Bay leaf (herb)	whole dried	sauces, casseroles, meat dishes
Caraway (spice)	whole seeds	cheese, bread, pickling, pork, vegetables
Cardamom (spice)	pod, whole seeds	Scandinavian baking, spiced wine, pudding
Celery seed (spice)	whole seeds	potato salad, pickles
Chervil (herb)	fresh, dried, ground	salads, sauces
Chives (herb)	fresh, dried, frozen	eggs, sour cream, salads, cottage cheese, dips
Cilantro (herb)	fresh	Mexican and Thai dishes, salsa
Cinnamon (spice)	whole sticks, ground	baking, meat, sauces, pickles, custards, cocoa
Cloves (spice)	whole, ground	hot beverages, ham, baked goods, vegetables
Coriander (spice)	whole seeds, ground	Scandinavian baking, pickling, curry blends
Cumin (spice)	whole seeds, ground	chili, curry, chili powder
Dill seed (spice)	whole seeds	dill pickles
Dill weed (herb)	fresh, dried	salads, vegetables, meat, fish, sauces
Fennel seed (spice)	whole seeds, ground	pickles, fish, meat, soup

Ginger (spice)		fresh, ground, dried	soups, curry, meat, baked goods
Mace (spice)		ground	fruit pies, puddings, baked goods, vegetables
Marjoram (herb)		fresh, dried, ground	salads, sauces, cooked green vegetables, meat
Mint (herb)		fresh, dried, ground	beverages, lamb, fruit, cooked vegetables, salads
Mustard (spice)		whole seeds, ground	sauces, pickling, dressings, meat, cheese dishes
Nutmeg (spice)		whole, ground	egg dishes, baked goods, custard, eggnog, fruit
Oregano (herb)		fresh, dried, ground	Italian dishes, pizza, cheese, vegetables, salads
Paprika (spice)		ground	used as garnish and in savory dishes, such as goulash
Parsley (herb)		fresh, dried	sauces, eggs, butter, fish, meat
Pepper, black and white (spice)		whole, ground	used in almost all types of savory dishes
Red cayenne pepper (spice)		ground	adds heat to vegetables, meat, eggs, sauces
Rosemary (herb)		fresh, dried, ground	soups, vegetables, meat, fish, eggs, dressings
Saffron (herb)		whole threads	Spanish breads, bouillabaisse, paella
Sage (herb)		fresh, dried, ground	cheese dishes, salad dressings, pork, beans
Savory (herb)		fresh, dried	pâtés, soups, meat, fish, beans
Tarragon (herb)		fresh, dried, ground	French dishes, sauces, chicken, fish
Thyme (herb)		fresh, dried, ground	vegetables, meat, soups, sauces
Turmeric (spice)		ground	curry, mustard, noodles, rice

OUTFITTING YOUR KITCHEN

Pots and Pans

When purchasing cookware for the stovetop, you probably have stood in the middle of the housewares department scratching your head. So many choices—which ones are right for you? Experts generally consider the best choice to be enameled cast iron, or heavy stainless steel with aluminum bottoms. Cast iron and aluminum are excellent heat conductors, but aluminum needs to be clad in another metal, such as stainless steel, so that it doesn't leach into the food. And an enamel coating makes cast iron easier to care for than uncoated cast iron.

Copper also is an excellent heat conductor. Copper pans are beautiful, but copper is expensive, high-maintenance and may be impractical. Regular stainless steel pans can cook "hot," and glass is not a good heat conductor.

Most pots and pans come in nonstick varieties. Nonstick pans are revered for their easy cleanup, but some may not get hot enough to sear foods, which is important when you need browned bits in the pan to make sauces and gravies. (Perhaps you could buy one skillet that is not nonstick for those uses.)

If you don't know a saucepan from a Dutch oven, here's a guide:

- **Saucepans:** A round pan with a handle and straight or flared sides. They are usually 4 quarts or smaller, have lids and are used for everything from cooking vegetables to making soups, sauces and cooked cereal.

- **Saucepots:** Larger than saucepans, saucepots are generally 5 quarts or larger, and are used primarily for cooking soups and stews. They generally have two handles toward the top of the pot and a tight-fitting lid. Also called Dutch ovens.

- **Skillets:** Also called frying pans, skillets are round, shallow pans with straight or sloping sides and long handles. They are used to fry or cook most any type of food from eggs to pork chops. They come in a wide range of sizes, but most cooks find the 8-, 10- and 12-inch pans to be the most useful.

Cookware for the Oven

Cookware for the oven includes those pans and baking dishes that are heat-resistant and are used in the oven for desserts, main courses, vegetables, roasting and casseroles. These include:

- **Baking Pans:** Used for desserts such as cakes and brownies. They are made of metal or glass and come in various shapes and sizes. The most popular sizes are 8- or 9-inch square and 13×9×2 inches.

• **Baking Sheets or Cookie Sheets:** Flat, metal sheets with one side. (Flat sheets with sides are called jellyroll pans and are especially for baking cakes for jellyrolls.) Baking sheets are primarily used for baked goods such as cookies and biscuits. Shiny sheets are usually preferred. Dark baking sheets are primarily used when a dark, crisp exterior is preferred; insulated baking sheets are a better choice for softer exteriors.

• **Casserole:** A deep, round or oval, ovenproof baking dish made from glass, ceramic or other heat-resistant material. Casseroles usually have two handles and tight-fitting lids.

• **Baking Dishes:** Shallow, glass or ceramic, heat-resistant dishes used for baking main dishes, side dishes and desserts. They are available in various shapes and sizes and often come with lids for easy reheating and storage.

• **Muffin Pans:** Used for baking muffins or cupcakes. Each pan has 6 or 12 cups ranging in size from miniature to jumbo.

• **Pie Pans:** Metal, glass or stoneware pans designed especially for baking pies. They are round, 9 or 10 inches in diameter, with flared sides to accommodate a pie crust. Deeper ones are called deep-dish pie pans.

Cookware for the Microwave

Microwave cookware is unique compared to regular stovetop and oven cookware. It is generally made from glass, plastic or ceramic, since metal can't be used in a microwave. Look for microwave cookware in sets that offer different sizes and shapes of containers suitable for microwave cooking.

Most microwave cookware will say "microwave-safe" or "suitable for microwave" or similar wording on the bottom of the dish. If you are not sure whether the cookware is microwavable, you can test it by filling a 1-cup glass measuring cup with water and placing it next to the container in question in the microwave. Turn the microwave on high for 1 minute. The water should be hot; the container in question should not be hot. If the container is hot to the touch, it is not microwave-safe. Microwave-safe cookware can be:

• **Glass:** It should be heat-resistant and able to withstand the heat generated from the microwave.

• **Plastic:** Most plasticware works great in the microwave oven. Look for labels indicating that plastic cookware is microwavable and dishwasher-safe, therefore able to withstand the heat.

• **Ceramic:** It should be unglazed because glazed ceramic pieces tend to absorb microwave energy too quickly, and can overheat and break.

STOCKING YOUR PANTRY

A well-stocked pantry makes it a snap to put together a wholesome meal your entire family will enjoy. Here are some suggestions for items to keep in your cupboard, refrigerator and freezer so that you aren't caught short at mealtime:

Pantry

Bagels, pita bread, muffins: for breakfast or sandwiches

Beans, canned and dried

Breadcrumbs: add filler to meatloaf and burgers, toppings for casseroles, coating for chicken, pork chops, fish

Campbell's® soups (including regular and 98% Fat Free and broths): great for a quick casserole or skillet meal

Campbell's® Turkey Gravy: for a fast hot sandwich and mashed potatoes

Campbell's® Tomato Juice

Canned fish, tuna and salmon

Chunky™ soup and chili varieties

Flour, all-purpose and whole-wheat

Fruits, canned and fresh: great for a quick snack or dessert

Herbs and spices, dried: great for flavor when fresh aren't available

Nonstick cooking spray

Oil: vegetable and olive oils

Onions

Pace® Salsa and Picante Sauces

Pasta, in a variety of shapes and sizes, egg noodles

Pepperidge Farm® Breads

Pepperidge Farm® assorted crackers, snacks and cookies

Pepperidge Farm® Goldfish®

Potatoes, white and sweet, instant mashed

Prego® Italian Sauces

		Freezer and Refrigerator	
Rice, quick-cooking and short-grain: for risotto and Asian dishes; long-grain white and brown: for fluffy rice dishes		Boneless, skinless chicken breasts	
Sauces, including barbecue, ketchup, soy, teriyaki		Canned breadsticks, rolls, pizza dough, biscuits	
Sugar, granulated and brown		Cheeses (shredded, sliced, ricotta, cottage): add to casseroles, homemade pizza, pasta dishes	
Swanson® Broth: (chicken, beef and vegetable broths): for homemade soups		Condiments, including salad dressings, yellow mustard, spicy mustard	
Tomatoes, canned			
V8® and V8 Splash® Juices		Fish fillets	
		Juices, including orange, grapefruit, lemon and lime	
Vegetables, canned and fresh		Lean beef, ground or roast	
Vinegar:			
White: for general use, pickling, dressings		Dairy products, including milk, yogurt, sour cream	
Balsamic: for salad dressings, flavoring fruits and vegetables		Pepperidge Farm® Puff Pastry: for quick, delicious desserts	
Flavored: for salad dressings, marinades, skillet meals		Vegetables and fruits, frozen and fresh	

FOOD SAFETY

We hear a lot about food safety these days, and with good reason—no one wants to cause foodborne illness. Here are some tips for keeping your family safe from foodborne bacteria:

• Refrigerators should be set no higher than 40°F. and freezers should be set at 0°F.

• Keep raw food, especially meats and fish, separate from cooked and ready-to-eat foods. (Perhaps you can designate a drawer or section of your refrigerator for raw foods.) To further prevent liquids from leaking onto other foods place on a tray or store on a low shelf. Do not store directly on the wire shelf.

• Defrost foods properly. Most of the time, frozen foods should be defrosted in the refrigerator. Some foods can be defrosted by the cold-water method: Wrap food in leak-proof plastic, and place it in a bowl or sink full of cold water for 20 to 30 minutes. Drain the water; then fill bowl or sink again with cold water. Repeat just until meat is thawed. Food can be defrosted in the microwave; however, foods should be cooked immediately when thawed this way (see pages 118 and 140).

• Use thawed foods within one or two days. Refrigerate thawed foods if you are not cooking them immediately after thawing. It is better not to refreeze them.

• Cook foods to proper temperatures (see temperature chart on page 21).

• Store foods properly. Leftovers should always be refrigerated promptly, particularly mayonnaise- and egg-based dishes, such as potato salad. Most leftovers are safest when consumed within about three days. Leftovers that need reheating should be heated to 165°F.

• Keep your hands—and your kitchen—clean. You don't need special cleansers or equipment. Consider using paper towels. Or, if using cloth towels or dishcloth or sponge, wash them often in the hot cycle of the washing machine. Clean all work surfaces, cutting boards, utensils, your sink and anything else that touched the food.

• If you are unsure about a food, discard it. Better safe than sorry.

Shopping for Fresh Meat, Poultry and Seafood

• Don't buy a torn or leaky package.

• Don't buy a package that is not cold to the touch.

• Don't buy food with an odor.

• If you know you won't be using meat within one or two days of the sell-by date, freeze it. Seafood doesn't keep as well as meat and should be used immediately or frozen.

Storing Fresh Meat, Poultry and Seafood

● Store in refrigerator or freezer as soon as possible in the coldest part of the refrigerator. In most refrigerators, that's the meat drawer.

● Wrap meat in additional plastic wrap before freezing because store wrapping can be permeable and may not keep the meat fresh.

Temperatures for Safe Cooking

To keep foods safe to eat for you and your family, always store and serve hot foods hot and cold foods cold. Use a food thermometer to test foods for doneness, using the guide below:

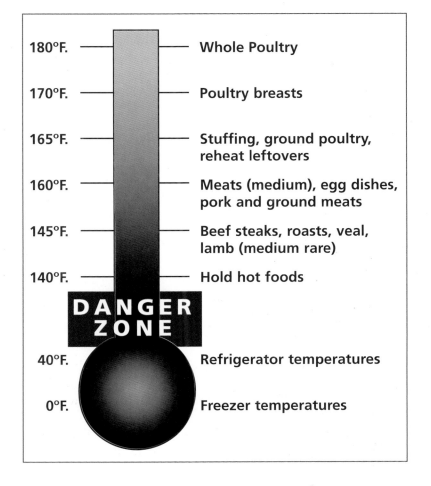

180°F.	Whole Poultry
170°F.	Poultry breasts
165°F.	Stuffing, ground poultry, reheat leftovers
160°F.	Meats (medium), egg dishes, pork and ground meats
145°F.	Beef steaks, roasts, veal, lamb (medium rare)
140°F.	Hold hot foods
	DANGER ZONE
40°F.	Refrigerator temperatures
0°F.	Freezer temperatures

SLOW COOKER TIPS

Slow cookers continue to be popular because they let you put together ingredients early in the day and come home to a hot, delicious wholesome meal. Here are a few things to remember when breaking out your slow cooker:

• For easy cleanup, spray the crock with nonstick cooking spray before adding the food. Or, try the new slow cooker liner bags. (To clean your slow cooker, follow the manufacturer's instructions.)

• Slow cookers cook best when they're two-thirds to three-quarters full. That's because most slow cookers' heating units are coiled inside the outer walls that surround the crockery insert rather than on the bottom of the crock.

• Keep a lid on it! The slow cooker can take as long as 20 minutes to regain the heat lost when the cover is removed. If the recipe calls for stirring or checking the dish near the end of the cooking time, replace the lid as quickly as you can. Otherwise, unless the recipe instructs you to remove the lid, don't, or food will take much longer to cook.

Adapting Recipes

If you'd like to adapt your favorite recipe to a slow cooker, find a similar slow cooker recipe. Note the cooking time and temperature, the amount of liquid, the quantity of meat and vegetables and how they're cut. Also note in what order the ingredients are added to the cooker. (Firmer vegetables, such as potatoes and carrots, sometimes go into the bottom of the cooker.) Because the slow cooker retains moisture, you may have to reduce the amount of liquid in a non-slow-cooker recipe by as much as half. Slow cooking tends to enhance the flavors of whole or fresh herbs, so use only about half the amount called for in the recipe. Add fresh herbs during the last half hour of cooking. Add dairy products at the end of cooking time so they do not curdle.

Selecting the Right Meat

Slow cookers are perfect for less tender cuts of meat. As a matter of fact, tender meat cuts, such as loin chops or filet mignon, will literally fall apart after a few hours in a slow cooker. Even the toughest cuts come out fork-tender and flavorful in a slow cooker, so save some money and pick the cheaper, less tender cuts such as round steak, chuck roast, lamb shanks, stew meats and others that require long cooking times.

Preparing Vegetables

Believe it or not, some vegetables can take longer to cook than meat. Pay careful attention to the recipe instructions so you're sure to cut vegetables in the proper size and add them to the slow cooker in the correct order. By the way, frozen vegetables should be thawed before adding to the slow cooker; frozen foods lower the temperature inside the cooker and can play havoc with cooking times.

Reducing Fat

Slow cooking can be reduced-fat cooking. First, less expensive cuts of meat that are perfect for the slow cooker are lower in fat than other cuts. When using fatty meats, try browning them first in a skillet on the stovetop before cooking in the slow cooker to cook away some of the fat.

Secondly, as we noted earlier, slow cookers retain moisture, so you don't have to begin with as much fat. Actually, much of the time, you don't have to begin with any fat; any flavorful liquid, such as Swanson® Broth, Campbell's® Soup, or Pace® Salsa or Picante Sauce, can stand in for fat and become an excellent sauce or gravy for the meal.

Food Safety Tips

If you do any advance preparation, such as trimming meat or cutting vegetables, make sure you keep the food covered and refrigerated until you're ready to add it to the cooker. Store uncooked meats and vegetables separately. After you've prepared raw meat, poultry or fish, remember to wash your cutting board, utensils, countertops, sink and hands with hot soapy water. (Many cooks have plastic cutting boards that they use just for meat preparation so they can wash and sterilize them in the dishwasher after use.)

Once your dish is cooked, serve it immediately. After serving, transfer food to a clean container, cover and refrigerate it immediately. Do not reheat leftovers in the slow cooker. Use a microwave oven, the range-top or the oven for reheating.

EMERGENCY SUBSTITUTIONS

When a recipe calls for:	In most cases, you may substitute:
1 cup fresh whole milk	1 cup 2%, 1% or skim milk, or ½ cup evaporated milk plus ½ cup water
1 cup half-and-half	1 cup less 2 tablespoons whole milk plus 2 tablespoons melted margarine or butter
1 clove garlic	⅛ teaspoon garlic powder or minced dried garlic
1 small onion	1 teaspoon onion powder or 1 tablespoon minced dried onion, rehydrated
1 teaspoon dry mustard	1 tablespoon prepared mustard
1 tablespoon cornstarch (for thickening)	2 tablespoons all-purpose flour or 2 teaspoons quick-cooking tapioca
1 cup sour cream	1 cup plain yogurt
1 tablespoon chopped fresh herbs	1 teaspoon dried herbs, crushed
½ cup granulated sugar	½ cup packed brown sugar
¼ cup honey	¼ cup light corn syrup
1 cup buttermilk	1 cup milk to which has been added 1 tablespoon lemon juice or white vinegar
1 egg whole	2 egg yolks or 3½ tablespoons egg substitute
1 egg white	2 tablespoons egg white substitute
1 teaspoon baking powder	¼ teaspoon baking soda plus ⅜ teaspoon cream of tartar
1 cup butter	1 cup margarine or ⅞ cup vegetable oil, lard or vegetable shortening
1 teaspoon vinegar	2 teaspoons lemon juice

PLANNING FOR A CROWD

Do you prepare way too much food for a party because you're afraid there won't be enough? Ever wondered if there was a formula or a guide to help you know how much food to prepare?

The amount of food you need depends on several things: how long the party will last and what kind of party it is (an all-afternoon Fourth of July picnic will require more food than a happy hour cocktail party), whether most of the people at the party are men or women (men eat more), even how rich or "special" the food is.

(Seafood will go faster than, say, hot dogs.) But no matter how carefully you calculate, you'll want to provide a few "filler" foods, such as breads, crackers, chips, dips, olives, pretzels, etc. to round things out—just in case. Here are some guidelines to help you figure out how much food you'll need for a gathering:

Course	Amount needed
Appetizers *(3 to 4 different types)*	10 to 12 per person for a cocktail party; 6 to 8, if a meal will be served
Beverages: Coffee or punch Soft drinks or tea Wine *(About 20 percent will not drink alcohol.)*	½ to 1 cup per person 1 to 2 cups per person ½ bottle per person
Casseroles	13×9×2-inch serves 12
Chili, stroganoff	5 to 6 ounces per person
Desserts: Brownies, bars Cookies	1 to 2 per person 2 to 3 per person
Pasta	3 to 4 ounces per person for sit-down dinner; 2 ounces per person for a buffet
Protein	5 to 6 ounces meat, fish or poultry per person (add slightly more for bone-in meats)
Side dishes: Green salad Vegetables Potato, macaroni salad Applesauce, cranberry sauce, etc.	1 head lettuce serves 5 3 to 4 ounces per person 3 ounces ½ cup per person
Soups, stews	1 cup per person (as first course) 1½ to 2 cups per person (as main dish)

FOOD EQUIVALENTS CHART

Bread and Cookies

2 slices bread	1 cup soft bread crumbs
2 slices bread	1 cup bread cubes
15 squares graham crackers	1 cup fine crumbs
22 vanilla wafers	1 cup fine crumbs

Dairy

1 pound butter	2 cups or 4 sticks 2 small tubs
1 cup heavy or whipping cream	2 cups whipped
8 ounces cream cheese	1 cup
1 pound Swiss or Cheddar cheese	4 cups shredded or grated
4 ounces blue cheese	1 cup crumbled
4 ounces Parmesan or Romano cheese	1¼ cups grated
1 large egg	3 tablespoons egg substitute

Dried legumes

1 cup dried beans or peas	2¼ cups cooked

Fruit

1 pound apples	3 medium
1 pound bananas	3 medium
1 medium lemon	2 tablespoons juice
1 medium orange	⅓ to ½ cup juice

Herbs

1 tablespoon chopped fresh	1 teaspoon dried, crumbled

Pasta

8 ounces elbow macaroni, uncooked	4 cups cooked
8 ounces spaghetti, uncooked	4 cups cooked
8 ounces medium noodles, uncooked	5 cups cooked

Rice

1 cup regular long-grain rice, uncooked	3 cups cooked
1 cup quick-cooking rice, uncooked	2 cups cooked

Vegetables

1 pound carrots	2½ cups sliced
1 pound cabbage	4 cups shredded
1 pound onions (yellow)	4 to 5 medium
1 medium onion	½ cup chopped
1 pound all-purpose potatoes	3 medium
1 pound fresh mushrooms	3 cups sliced
1 pound tomatoes	3 medium
1 pound broccoli	2 cups flowerets

Miscellaneous

1 pound cooked meat	3 cups diced
1 pound raw boneless meat	2 cups cubed cooked
1 pound raw ground beef	2¾ cups cooked

Appetizers

START TO FINISH:
2 hours, 15 minutes

Thawing: 40 minutes
Prepping: 15 minutes
Baking: 20 minutes
Standing: 1 hour

Brie en Croûte

Makes 12 servings

½ of a 17.3 ounce package Pepperidge Farm® Frozen Puff
  Pastry Sheets (1 sheet)
1 egg
1 tablespoon water
¼ cup toasted sliced almonds (optional)
¼ cup chopped fresh parsley
1 (1 pound) Brie cheese round
  Pepperidge Farm® Water Crackers

1. Thaw the pastry sheet at room temperature for 40 minutes or
until it's easy to handle. Heat the oven to 400°F. Lightly grease a
baking sheet. Stir the egg and water with a fork in cup.

2. Unfold the pastry sheet on a lightly floured surface. Roll the
sheet into a 14-inch square. (Cut off the corners to make a circle.)

3. Center the almonds and parsley on the pastry. Top with the
cheese. Brush the edge of the pastry with the egg mixture. Fold two
opposite sides over the cheese. Trim the remaining two sides to
2 inches from the edge of cheese. Fold these two sides onto the
cheese. Press edges to seal. Place seam-side down on the baking
sheet. Decorate the top with pastry scraps if desired. Brush with
the egg mixture.

4. Bake for 20 minutes or until golden. Let stand for 1 hour before
serving. Serve with the crackers.

Tex-Mex Toasts

Makes 6 servings

START TO FINISH:
22 minutes

Prepping: 20 minutes
Baking: 2 minutes

Cooking for a Crowd:
Recipe may be doubled.

1 package (9.5 ounces) Pepperidge Farm® Mozzarella & Monterey Jack Cheese Texas Toast

6 tablespoons Pace® Refried Beans

Pace® Chunky Salsa, any variety

Sour cream (optional)

Chopped green onions (optional)

1. Prepare the toast according to the package directions.

2. Spread **1 tablespoon** of the beans on each toast slice. Bake for 2 minutes more or until hot.

3. Top each toast slice with salsa, sour cream and green onions, if desired.

Warm Cheesy Chili Dip

Makes 12 servings

1 **package (8 ounces) cream cheese**
1 **can (16 ounces) Campbell's® Chunky™ Hold The Beans Chili**
⅓ **cup shredded Mexican blend cheese**
2 **tablespoons sliced pitted ripe olives**
1 **medium green onion, sliced (about 2 tablespoons)**
1 **tablespoon chopped fresh cilantro leaves**
   Tortilla chips

START TO FINISH:
3 minutes

Prepping: 2 minutes
Microwaving:
  1 minute

Leftover Tip:
Use leftover dip as a cheesy hot topping for steamed broccoli or cauliflower.

1. Unwrap the cream cheese and place it on a microwavable serving plate. Top with the chili and cheese blend.

2. Microwave on HIGH for 45 seconds to 1 minute or until the chili is hot and the cheese blend melts. Top with the olives, green onion and cilantro.

3. Serve with the chips for dipping.

Appetizing Ideas

Appetizers whet the appetite and prepare your palate for the meal to come. Whether you're preparing little bites to tide the family over until the meal's ready or you're making fancy hors d'oeuvres for a party, tasty meal-starters can kick off your meal just right. Here are some tips for successful appetizers:

• Appetizers are beginning to include light first courses, but traditionally, they are finger foods. That means you don't have to worry about providing much more than small plates and napkins. Tortilla chips with Pace® salsa, cheese dips and layered spreads are perfect examples of finger foods easy for the cook and the guest.

• Plan your appetizer menu around the seasons. A cool dip is perfect before a summer barbecue, while a hearty appetizer paves the way for a cold-weather, Super Bowl party.

• Try an appetizer buffet, arranged on the dining room table or kitchen counter or island.

For large crowds, set up buffets in several places in your kitchen or dining room to manage the flow of guests. Serving buffet-style is easier than carrying trays of food through the crowd, and guests gathered around a buffet table encourages talk and fun.

• Make sure there are a variety of flavors, textures and colors. Balance a platter of cold, crisp, raw veggies and Garden Vegetable Spread with a hot nacho dip and chips, for example.

• Keep things simple and easy for yourself and your guests: Serve napkins, breads or chips in baskets. Stand silverware in large, colorful glasses. Serve beverages in easy-pour pitchers.

• Need more color on your appetizer table? Try garnishes. Lemon or lime slices, fresh flowers, greens or fresh herbs all add color and entice guests to try your yummy food.

Caponata Appetizer

Makes 5 cups

START TO FINISH:
1 hour, 10 minutes

Prepping: 15 minutes
Cooking: 55 minutes

Leftover Tip:
Leftover caponata is delicious tossed with hot cooked pasta topped off with some grated Parmesan cheese.

1 tablespoon vegetable oil

1 large eggplant, cut into cubes (about 8 cups)

1 Spanish onion, chopped (about 2 cups)

1 large red pepper, chopped (about 1 cup)

2 cloves garlic, minced

1 can (10¾ ounces) Campbell's® Condensed Tomato Soup

1⅓ cups water

1 teaspoon dried oregano leaves, crushed

Pepperidge Farm® Cracker Quartet **or** Cracker Trio Entertaining Collection Cracker Assortment

1. Heat the oil in a 6-quart saucepot over medium-high heat. Add the eggplant, onion, pepper and garlic and cook for 10 minutes or until the eggplant begins to soften, stirring often.

2. Add the soup and water and heat the mixture to a boil. Cover and reduce the heat to low. Cook for 40 minutes or until the vegetables are tender.

3. Stir in the oregano. Serve warm or at room temperature with the crackers.

Garden Vegetable Spread

Makes 1½ cups

1 package (8 ounces) cream cheese, softened

1 teaspoon lemon juice

¼ teaspoon dried dill weed, crushed **or** 1 teaspoon chopped fresh dill weed

½ cup chopped cucumber

1 medium carrot, shredded (about ½ cup)

1 medium green onion, chopped (about 2 tablespoons)

Pepperidge Farm® Three Cracker Assortment

**START TO FINISH:
2 hours, 10 minutes**

Prepping: 10 minutes
Refrigerating: 2 hours

1. Stir the cheese until it's smooth in a small bowl. Stir in the lemon juice, dill, cucumber, carrot and green onion. Refrigerate the mixture for 2 hours or until flavors are blended.

2. Serve with the crackers.

Hot Artichoke Dip

Makes 3 cups

START TO FINISH:
40 minutes

Prepping: 10 minutes
Baking: 30 minutes

1 cup mayonnaise

1 cup sour cream

1 can (14 ounces) artichoke hearts, drained and chopped

¼ cup chopped roasted sweet peppers

¼ cup grated Parmesan cheese

1 can (2.8 ounces) French fried onions (1⅓ cups)

Assorted Pepperidge Farm® Crackers

1. Heat the oven to 375°F. Stir the mayonnaise, sour cream, artichokes, peppers, cheese and ⅔ **cup** of the onions in a 9-inch pie plate or 1-quart baking dish.

2. Bake for 25 minutes or until hot.

3. Sprinkle with the remaining onions. Bake for 5 minutes more or until golden.

4. Serve with the crackers for dipping.

Italiano Fondue

Makes 2 cups

1¾ cups Prego® Traditional Italian Sauce
¼ cup dry red wine
1 cup shredded mozzarella cheese (4 ounces)
Suggested Dippers: Warm Pepperidge Farm® Garlic Bread, cut into cubes, meatballs, sliced cooked Italian pork sausage, breaded mozzarella sticks **and/or** whole mushrooms

**START TO FINISH:
20 minutes**

Prepping: 5 minutes
Cooking: 10 minutes
Standing: 5 minutes

1. Stir the Italian sauce and wine in a 1-quart saucepan. Heat to a boil over medium heat, stirring often. Cook for 5 minutes for the alcohol to evaporate.

2. Pour the sauce into a fondue pot or slow cooker. Stir in the cheese. Let stand for 5 minutes for cheese to melt slightly.

3. Serve warm with *Suggested Dippers*.

Layered Pizza Dip

Makes about 3 cups

START TO FINISH:
30 minutes

Prepping: 10 minutes
Baking: 15 minutes
Cooling: 5 minutes

Easy Substitution Tip:
Substitute or add any of the following toppings for the pepperoni: sliced pitted ripe olives, sliced mushrooms, chopped sweet peppers or chopped onions.

1 cup part-skim ricotta cheese
½ cup chopped pepperoni
1 cup shredded mozzarella cheese
  (4 ounces)
1 cup Prego® Italian Sauce, any variety
  Pepperidge Farm® Frozen Garlic Bread, any variety, heated according to package directions **or** Pepperidge Farm® Crackers, any variety

1. Spread the ricotta cheese in an even layer in a 9-inch pie plate. Top with ¼ **cup** of the pepperoni and ½ **cup** of the mozzarella cheese. Carefully spread the Italian sauce over the cheese. Sprinkle with the remaining pepperoni and mozzarella cheese.

2. Bake at 375°F. for 15 minutes or until hot. Let cool for 5 minutes.

3. Serve with the garlic bread or crackers for dipping.

Salsa Party Meatballs

Makes 30 appetizers

2½ pounds ground beef **or** ground meat loaf mix
(beef, pork, veal)

¼ cup milk

6 tablespoons dry bread crumbs

2 eggs

1 teaspoon garlic powder

4 medium green onions, chopped (about ½ cup)

1 cup shredded Cheddar cheese (4 ounces)

2 tablespoons olive **or** vegetable oil

2 jars (16 ounces **each**) Pace® Chunky Salsa

**START TO FINISH:
35 minutes**

Prepping: 10 minutes
Cooking: 25 minutes

1. Thoroughly mix the beef, milk, bread crumbs, eggs, garlic powder, green onions and **2 tablespoons** of the cheese in a large bowl. Shape the mixture firmly into 30 (1½-inch) meatballs.

2. Heat the oil in 12-inch nonstick skillet over medium-high heat. Add the meatballs in 2 batches and cook until they're well browned. Remove the meatballs with a slotted spoon and set them aside. Pour off any fat.

3. Stir the salsa into the skillet. Heat to a boil. Return the meatballs to the skillet and reduce the heat to low. Cover and cook for 8 minutes or until the meatballs are cooked through*.

4. Stir the remaining cheese into the skillet and cook for 1 minute more or until the cheese melts. Sprinkle with additional chopped green onions if desired.

*The internal temperature of the meatballs should reach 160°F.

Single-Serve Southwest Dip Cups

Makes 24 servings

START TO FINISH:
20 minutes

Prepping: 20 minutes

Campbell's Kitchen Tip:
Stop traffic jams around the dip bowl! Spoon a few tablespoons of favorite dips into foil baking cups. Your guests can cruise by the serving table and pick up a dip cup and some dippers and move on to mingle with other guests.

24 (2½-inch) foil baking cups
 1 can (15.5 ounces) Pace® Refried Beans
 2 jars (11 ounces **each**) Pace® Chunky Salsa
 3 medium avocados, seeded, peeled and chopped (about 1½ cups)
1½ cups shredded Cheddar cheese (6 ounces)
1½ cups sour cream
 ½ cup chopped fresh cilantro leaves
   Bite-size tortilla chips for dipping

1. Place the foil cups on a serving platter.

2. Layer **about 1 tablespoon each** of the beans, salsa, avocado and cheese into **each** cup. Top each with a spoonful of sour cream and sprinkle with cilantro. Serve with the chips for dipping.

Swiss Cheese Fondue

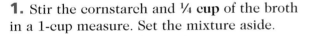

Makes 6 servings

- **1 tablespoon cornstarch**
- **1 cup Swanson® Chicken Broth (Regular, Natural Goodness™ or Certified Organic)**
- **1 clove garlic, cut in half**
- **½ cup dry white wine**
- **1 tablespoon lemon juice**
- **1 pound natural aged Swiss cheese (Emmentaler, Natural Gruyère or raclette cheese) shredded, at room temperature**
- **¼ teaspoon ground nutmeg**
- **Ground black pepper**
- **1 loaf (about 1 pound) French bread, cut into cubes or cut up fresh vegetables**

START TO FINISH:
25 minutes

Prepping: 5 minutes
Cooking: 20 minutes

Cooking for a Crowd:
Recipe may be doubled.

1. Stir the cornstarch and ¼ **cup** of the broth in a 1-cup measure. Set the mixture aside.

2. Rub a 2-quart saucepan or fondue pot with the garlic. Discard the garlic.

3. Add remaining broth and wine to the saucepan. Heat over medium heat until hot but not bubbling. Add the lemon juice. Add the cheese, a little at a time, stirring until the cheese melts before adding more.

4. Stir the cornstarch mixture and stir it into the saucepan. Heat to a boil. Reduce the heat to low. Cook and stir for 1 minute. Add the nutmeg and black pepper to taste. Keep warm in a fondue pot. Serve with the bread or vegetables for dipping.

Beverages

START TO FINISH:
4 hours, 15 minutes

Prepping: 15 minutes
Refrigerating: 4 hours

Cooking for a Crowd:
Recipe may be doubled.

Splashy Sangria

Makes 8 servings

  3 cups V8 Splash® Tropical Blend Juice
  1 bottle (750 ml) Cabernet Sauvignon **or** other dry red
     wine (3 cups)
 ¼ cup sugar
  1 orange, thinly sliced
  1 lemon, thinly sliced
  1 lime, thinly sliced
  2 cups seltzer

1. Stir the juice, wine, sugar and the orange, lemon and lime slices in a 3-quart pitcher. Refrigerate for at least 4 hours or overnight, stirring occasionally to dissolve sugar.

2. Stir in the seltzer just before serving.

Splash & Rainbow Punch

Makes 1 serving

START TO FINISH:
5 minutes

Prepping: 5 minutes

Campbell's Kitchen Tip:

It is helpful to use a melon baller for scooping the sorbet.

½ cup **Diet V8 Splash**®, any flavor, chilled

½ cup **sparkling mineral water or seltzer**, chilled

⅓ cup **assorted flavors sorbet (lime, raspberry, strawberry, peach, lemon and/or mango)**

Put the juice and mineral water into a tall glass. Scoop the sorbet and put in the glass. Serve immediately.

Bellini Splash

Makes 2 servings

START TO FINISH:
5 minutes

Prepping: 5 minutes

½ cup **V8 Splash**® **Peach Lemonade or Mango Peach**, chilled

¼ cup **peach nectar**, chilled

1 cup **champagne, sparkling wine or sparkling cider,** chilled

Stir the juice and nectar in a 1-cup measure. Divide between 2 fluted champagne glasses. Pour in champagne. Serve immediately.

Third-Down Tropical Mojitos

Makes 8 servings

1 **cup fresh mint leaves**

    Ice cubes

3 **bottles (16 fluid ounces each) V8 Splash® Tropical Blend Juice (6 cups), chilled**

1 **cup (8 fluid ounces) rum**

1. Divide the mint leaves among 8 tall glasses. Mash lightly with the back of a spoon. Fill the glasses with ice.

2. Stir the juice and rum in a 2-quart pitcher. Pour over the ice-filled glasses.

START TO FINISH:
10 minutes

Prepping: 10 minutes

Cooking for a Crowd:
Recipe may be doubled.

Cool & Creamy Fruit Smoothies

Makes 2 servings

**START TO FINISH:
10 minutes**

Prepping: 10 minutes

1 cup V8 Splash® Smoothies Strawberry Banana Juice
½ cup peach sorbet **or** your favorite flavor
½ cup vanilla lowfat yogurt
½ cup fresh strawberries cut into quarters

Put the juice, sorbet, yogurt and strawberries in an electric blender container. Cover and blend until smooth. Serve immediately.

Frosted Citrus Green Tea

Makes 6 servings

2 **bottles (16 fluid ounces each)** Diet V8 Splash® Tropical Blend Juice (4 cups), chilled

4 **cups water**

8 **green tea bags**

Fresh mint sprigs (optional)

Lemon wedges (optional)

1. Pour **2 cups** juice into **1** ice cube tray. Freeze for 1 hour, 30 minutes or until the mixture is frozen.

2. Heat the water in a 2-quart saucepan over high heat to a boil. Remove the pan from the heat. Add the tea bags and let them steep for 5 minutes. Remove the tea bags.

3. Stir the tea and the remaining juice in an 8-cup measure. Refrigerate for at least 1 hour, 30 minutes.

4. Unmold the cubes from the tray and place 3 to 4 cubes in each of 6 tall glasses. Divide the tea mixture among the glasses. Serve with mint and lemon, if desired.

**START TO FINISH:
1 hour, 40 minutes**

Prepping: 10 minutes
Freezing/Refrigerating:
1 hour, 30 minutes

Beverages

Cooking for a Crowd:
Recipe may be doubled.

Frosty Fruit Cooler

Makes 2 servings

START TO FINISH:
10 minutes

Prepping: 10 minutes

1 cup V8 Splash® Orange Pineapple Juice
¼ cup vanilla yogurt
½ cup cut-up strawberries **or** raspberries
½ cup ice cubes

Put the juice, yogurt, strawberries and ice cubes in an electric blender container. Cover and blend until smooth. Serve immediately.

Mulled Raspberry Mosas

Makes 4 servings

 16 fresh **or** thawed frozen raspberries
1⅓ cup V8 Splash® Guava Passion Fruit Juice, chilled
  1 cup champagne **or** seltzer, chilled

1. Place **4** raspberries in each of 4 stemmed glasses. Mash lightly with a fork.

2. Pour ⅓ **cup** juice and ¼ **cup** champagne in each glass. Stir. Serve immediately.

START TO FINISH:
10 minutes

Prepping: 10 minutes

Beverages

Cooking for a Crowd:
Recipe may be doubled.

Spicy Mary Martini

Makes 2 servings

START TO FINISH:
5 minutes

Prepping: 5 minutes

2 cans (5.5 fluid ounces **each**) V8® Spicy Hot Vegetable Juice

3 fluid ounces (6 tablespoons) pepper-flavored vodka

Dash chipotle hot pepper sauce (or to taste)

2 cups ice cubes

Seasoned salt (optional)

2 stalks celery

Put the juice, vodka, pepper sauce and ice in a cocktail shaker. Cover and shake until blended. Strain into 2 chilled tall glasses rimmed with seasoned salt, if desired. Serve with the celery.

Drink Up!

Whether entertaining for many or just a few, plan beverages just as you plan the food. Here are some tips:

• You can get about 30 (5-ounce) servings from an average size punch bowl.

• Many punch-type drinks can be made ahead and chilled. But hold off on adding the sparkling water, wine or soda until just before serving so the punch doesn't lose the fizz by the time guests arrive. Likewise, wait to add the fresh fruit garnishes, ice rings or ice cubes until you're ready to serve.

• Label alcoholic and nonalcoholic drinks so guests will know the difference. Use placecards or perhaps prepare the drinks in different colors to distinguish them.

• As a substitute for granulated sugar for hot tea, serve cinnamon imperials, lemon drops, peppermint candies or multi-colored candied sugar.

• Dip the rims of iced tea glasses into lemon juice and then into sugar before adding tea. Add some frozen berries, fresh mint or citrus slices.

• Try serving V8® Vegetable Juice in glasses that have been dipped in lemon juice, then celery salt. Use green onions or celery stalks as stirrers.

• Jazz up after-dinner coffee with a dash of nutmeg, ginger or cardamom, or with a cinnamon stick.

Berry Rum Toddies

Makes 8 servings

4 bottles (16 fluid ounces **each**) V8 Splash® Berry Blend Juice (8 cups)

1 cup (8 fluid ounces) dark spiced **or** regular rum

2 teaspoons ground cinnamon

1¼ teaspoons ground ginger

8 cinnamon sticks

1. Heat the juice, rum, cinnamon and ginger in a 3-quart saucepan over medium-high heat to a boil and cook for 5 minutes, stirring occasionally.

2. Place **1** cinnamon stick in each of 8 mugs. Divide the juice mixture among the mugs. Serve immediately.

START TO FINISH:
10 minutes

Prepping/Cooking:
10 minutes

Cooking for a Crowd:
Recipe may be doubled.

Beverages

Soups and Stews

START TO FINISH:
2 hours, 45 minutes

Prepping: 1 hour
Cooking: 1 hour,
45 minutes

Sausage & Escarole Soup

Makes 6 servings

- 1 cup dried navy beans
- 1 pound sweet Italian pork sausage, casing removed
- 1 large onion, thinly sliced (about 1 cup)
- 2 cloves garlic, thinly sliced
- 6 cups Swanson® Chicken Broth (Regular, Natural Goodness™ **or** Certified Organic)
- 1 head escarole (about 1 pound), chopped (about 8 cups)
  Grated Parmesan cheese
  Freshly ground black pepper

1. Soak the beans according to the package directions. Drain.

2. Cook the sausage in a 4-quart saucepan over medium-high heat until the sausage is well browned, stirring frequently to break up meat. Remove the sausage with a slotted spoon and set it aside.

3. Add the onion and cook for 2 minutes. Add the garlic and cook for 30 seconds.

4. Stir the broth and the beans into the saucepan. Heat to a boil. Cover and cook over low heat for 1 hour, 30 minutes or until the beans are tender.

5. Add the escarole. Return the sausage to the pan. Cover and cook for 5 minutes or until the escarole is tender. Serve the soup with the cheese and black pepper.

Creamy Citrus Tomato Soup with Pesto Croutons

Makes 6 servings

START TO FINISH:
15 minutes

Prepping: 10 minutes
Cooking: 5 minutes

Campbell's Kitchen Tip:
The flavor and texture of goat cheese would be a great addition here. If you have some on hand, spread a little goat cheese on the toast slice before topping with the pesto.

1 can (10¾ ounces) Campbell's® Condensed Tomato Soup
1 cup milk
½ cup light cream **or** half-and-half
1 tablespoon lemon juice
6 tablespoons prepared pesto
6 slices French **or** Italian bread, ½-inch thick, toasted

1. Stir the soup, milk, cream and lemon juice in a 2-quart saucepan. Heat the soup over medium heat until hot.

2. Spread **1 tablespoon** of the pesto on each toast slice.

3. Divide the soup among 6 serving bowls. Float a pesto crouton on each bowl of soup.

Herb-Simmered Beef Stew

Makes 6 servings

2 pounds beef for stew, cut into 1-inch pieces
Ground black pepper

2 tablespoons all-purpose flour

2 tablespoons olive oil

3 cups thickly sliced mushrooms (about 8 ounces)

3 cloves garlic, minced

½ teaspoon **each** dried marjoram, thyme **and** rosemary leaves, crushed **or** 1½ teaspoons **each** chopped fresh marjoram, thyme **and** rosemary

1 bay leaf

1¾ cups Swanson® Beef Broth (Regular, Lower Sodium **or** Certified Organic)

3 cups fresh **or** frozen baby carrots

12 whole baby red-skinned potatoes, with a strip of peel removed in center

START TO FINISH:
1 hour, 45 minutes

Prepping: 15 minutes
Cooking: 1 hour, 30 minutes

1. Sprinkle the beef with the black pepper. Lightly coat the beef with the flour.

2. Heat the oil in a 4-quart saucepan over medium-high heat. Add the beef in 2 batches and cook until it's well browned on all sides, stirring often. Remove the beef with a slotted spoon and set it aside.

3. Add the mushrooms, garlic, marjoram, thyme, rosemary and bay leaf and cook until the mushrooms are tender and the liquid is evaporated.

4. Stir the broth into the saucepan. Heat to a boil. Return the beef to the pan and reduce the heat to low. Cover and cook for 45 minutes.

5. Add the carrots and potatoes. Cover and cook for 30 minutes more or until the meat and vegetables are fork-tender. Stir the stew occasionally while cooking. Remove the bay leaf.

Corn & Red Pepper Chowder

Makes 6 servings

START TO FINISH:
50 minutes

Prepping: 5 minutes
Cooking: 45 minutes

2 **tablespoons canola oil**

1 **large sweet onion, diced (about 2 cups)**

¼ **cup all-purpose flour**

2 **cloves garlic, minced**

6 **cups Swanson® Chicken Broth (Regular, Natural Goodness™ or Certified Organic)**

2 **medium Yukon gold potatoes, diced (about 2 cups)**

2 **cups fresh corn kernels or 1 package (10 ounces) frozen whole kernel corn**

1 **jar (7 ounces) roasted red peppers, drained and chopped**

½ **cup heavy cream (optional)**

⅓ **cup chopped fresh basil leaves**

1. Heat the oil in a 4-quart saucepan over medium heat. Add the onion and cook until tender. Stir in the flour and garlic. Cook and stir for 1 minute.

2. Stir the broth and potatoes into the saucepan. Cook and stir until the mixture boils and thickens. Reduce the heat to low. Cook for 20 minutes or until the potatoes are tender.

3. Stir in the corn and pepper. Cook for 10 minutes more.

4. Add the cream, if desired and ¼ **cup** basil. Season to taste. Divide the soup among 6 serving bowls. Sprinkle each serving of soup with the remaining basil.

Chipotle Black Bean Soup with Avocado Cream

Makes 8 servings

2 tablespoons olive oil

4 large carrots, diced (about 2 cups)

1 large sweet onion, diced (about 2 cups)

2 cloves garlic, minced

1 canned chipotle pepper in adobo sauce, minced*

4 cups Swanson® Chicken Broth (Regular, Natural Goodness™ **or** Certified Organic)

3 cans (about 15 ounces **each**) black beans, rinsed and drained

1 small ripe avocado, pitted, peeled and cut into cubes (about ½ cup)

¼ cup sour cream

1 tablespoon lemon juice

2 tablespoons chopped fresh cilantro leaves

START TO FINISH:
50 minutes

Prepping: 10 minutes
Cooking: 40 minutes

1. Heat the oil in a 4-quart saucepan. Add the carrots and onion and cook until tender-crisp. Add the garlic and pepper and cook for 1 minute.

2. Add the broth and beans. Heat to a boil. Reduce the heat to low. Cook for 25 minutes.

3. Mash the avocado with a fork in a small bowl until smooth. Stir in the sour cream, lemon juice and cilantro and set it aside.

4. Spoon ⅓ the soup mixture into an electric blender container. Cover and blend until smooth. Pour puréed soup into saucepan. Repeat the blending process with the remaining soup. Season to taste. Divide the soup among 8 serving bowls. Top each serving of soup with the avocado cream.

*For a less spicy soup, use **half** of a chipotle pepper.*

Soups and Stews

Howlin' Coyote Chili

Makes 6 servings

**START TO FINISH:
50 minutes**

Prepping: 15 minutes
Cooking: 35 minutes

Easy Substitution Tip:
Use cooked turkey
instead of chicken and
try Cheddar or
Monterey Jack cheese
for a milder taste.

2 **tablespoons olive oil**
1 **large onion, chopped (about 1 cup)**
1 **stalk celery, chopped (about ½ cup)**
1 **small red pepper, chopped (about ½ cup)**
3 **tablespoons all-purpose flour**
1 **tablespoon ground cumin**
2 **cups Swanson® Chicken Broth (Regular, Natural Goodness™
    or Certified Organic)**
2 **cans (about 15 ounces each) white Northern beans,
    drained**
1 **jar (16 ounces) Pace® Chipotle Chunky Salsa**
2 **cups chopped cooked chicken**
    Shredded pepper Jack cheese
    Cubed avocado

1. Heat the oil in a 6-quart saucepot over medium-high heat. Add the onion, celery and pepper. Cook and stir until the vegetables are tender.

2. Stir in the flour and cumin. Cook and stir for 2 minutes. Slowly stir in the broth. Cook and stir until the mixture boils and thickens.

3. Add the beans, salsa and chicken. Heat to a boil. Reduce the heat to low. Cook for 20 minutes. Serve the chili with cheese and avocado.

Soup's On!

Need a meal in a hurry? Why not make it
a soup buffet night? Just heat up some
Campbell's® Chunky™ Chili, Campbell's®
Chunky Soup or Campbell's® Tomato Soup,
and set up a buffet of toppings and
accompaniments so each member of the family
can customize his or her own bowl of soup. Round out the meal with
a quick green salad and some Goldfish® crackers or Pepperidge
Farm® croutons, and you've got a meal.

Hearty Vegetarian Chili

Makes 4 servings

   1 tablespoon vegetable oil
   1 large onion, chopped (about 1 cup)
   1 large green pepper, chopped (about 1 cup)
   1 tablespoon chili powder
   ½ teaspoon ground cumin
   ¼ teaspoon garlic powder **or** 2 cloves garlic, minced
   2½ cups V8® 100% Vegetable Juice
   1 can (about 15 ounces) black **or** kidney beans, rinsed and drained
   1 can (about 15 ounces) pinto beans, rinsed and drained

**START TO FINISH:
30 minutes**

Prepping: 10 minutes
Cooking: 20 minutes

Leftover Tip:

Reheat leftover chili and serve as a topping for baked potatoes.

Soups and Stews

1. Heat the oil in a 4-quart saucepan over medium heat. Add the onion, pepper, chili powder, cumin and garlic powder and cook until the vegetables are tender, stirring often.

2. Stir the vegetable juice into the saucepan. Heat to a boil. Reduce the heat to low. Cover and cook for 5 minutes.

3. Stir in the beans and heat through.

Soup Buffet Toppings:

- Chopped baby spinach leaves
- Chopped bell peppers (red, yellow and green)
- Chopped fresh herbs (parsley, chives or cilantro)
- Cooked white rice
- Crumbled cooked bacon
- Crumbled tortilla or corn chips
- Pepperidge Farm® Goldfish® crackers
- Grated Parmesan or Parmesan & Romano cheese blend
- Hot pepper sauce
- Jalapeño pepper slices
- Oyster crackers or bagel chips
- Pace® Salsa
- Pepperidge Farm® croutons
- Prepared pesto sauce
- Shredded cheese (Cheddar, Monterey Jack and/or Colby)
- Sliced green onions
- Sliced ripe olives
- Sour cream
- Whole kernel corn

And, on nights when you have more time, try serving your soup or chili over:

- Baked Potatoes
- Biscuits
- Garlic Bread slices
- Pasta
- Rice

Spring Pea & Mint Soup

Makes 6 servings

START TO FINISH:
55 minutes

Prepping: 10 minutes
Cooking: 45 minutes

1 tablespoon butter

1 tablespoon vegetable oil

3 small leeks, whites only, cleaned and diced (about 2 cups)

4 cups Swanson® Chicken Broth (Regular, Natural Goodness™ **or** Certified Organic)

1 medium Yukon Gold potato, diced (about 1 cup)

1 package (16 ounces) frozen peas (3 cups)

½ cup heavy cream **or** crème fraiche

¼ cup thinly sliced fresh mint leaves

1 cup Pepperidge Farm® Croutons, any variety

1. Heat the butter and oil in a 3-quart saucepan over medium heat. Add the leeks and cook until tender.

2. Stir the broth and potato into the saucepan. Heat to a boil. Reduce the heat to low. Cook for 20 minutes or until the potato is tender.

3. Stir in the peas. Cook for 10 minutes or until the peas are tender.

4. Spoon ⅓ of the soup mixture into an electric blender container. Cover and blend until smooth. Pour puréed soup into saucepan. Repeat the blending process with the remaining soup.

5. Stir the cream and mint into the soup mixture. Cook over medium heat until it's hot. Season to taste. Divide the soup among 6 serving bowls. Top each serving of soup with croutons.

Souper Pastry Bowls

Makes 2 servings

½ **of a 17.3 ounce package Pepperidge Farm® Frozen Puff Pastry Sheets (1 sheet)**

Assorted fresh herb leaves (rosemary, thyme or sage), optional

1 **egg**

1 **tablespoon water**

1 **can (18.6 to 19 ounces) Campbell's® Chunky™ Soup or Chili, any variety**

START TO FINISH:
1 hour, 10 minutes

Thawing: 40 minutes
Prepping: 10 minutes
Baking: 20 minutes

1. Thaw the pastry sheet at room temperature for 40 minutes or until it's easy to handle. Heat the oven to 400°F.

2. Unfold the pastry sheet on a lightly floured surface. Roll the sheet into an 18×9-inch rectangle and cut it in half crosswise to form 2 (9-inch) squares. Gently press the dough with lightly floured fingers into 2 (16-ounce) oven-safe bowls and fold over the corners to form a rim. Gently press the herb leaves into the dough, if desired.

3. Stir the egg and water with a fork in a small cup. Brush the dough with the egg mixture. Bake for 20 minutes or until the pastry is golden and puffed in the center. Let the pastry cool for 5 minutes.

4. Meanwhile, heat the soup or chili according to the package directions.

5. Using a small knife, cut a slit in the puffed center of the pastry and gently push down to form a bowl. Divide the soup evenly between the pastry bowls and serve immediately.

Campbell's Kitchen Tip:
Take a short cut with the pastry bowls. Bake off 1 package (10 ounces) Pepperidge Farm® Frozen Puff Pastry Shells according to package directions in place of the Pepperidge Farm® Puff Pastry Sheet. Then place each baked shell on a serving plate or in small bowls, gently push in the pastry centers and divide the heated soup or chili among shells just before serving.

Soups and Stews

Spinach Egg Drop Soup with Ham

Makes 10 servings

START TO FINISH:
25 minutes

Prepping: 10 minutes
Cooking: 15 minutes

Time-Saving Tip:
To thaw the spinach, microwave on HIGH for 3 minutes, breaking apart with a fork halfway through heating.

8 cups Swanson® Chicken Broth (Regular, Natural Goodness™ or Certified Organic)

1 package (16 ounces) frozen chopped spinach, thawed and drained

1 cup diced cooked ham (about 4 ounces)

2 eggs, beaten

¼ cup grated Parmesan cheese
    Dash ground nutmeg

1. Heat **7 cups** of the broth, spinach and ham in a 4-quart saucepan over medium-high heat to a boil. Reduce the heat to medium.

2. Beat the eggs, cheese and nutmeg with a fork in a small bowl. Beat the remaining broth into the egg mixture.

3. While stirring the broth mixture in one direction, slowly pour the egg mixture in a steady stream into the broth. Cook and stir until the eggs are set.

Spicy Verde Chicken & Bean Chili

Makes 6 servings

2 tablespoons butter

1 large onion, chopped (about 1 cup)

¼ teaspoon garlic powder **or** 2 cloves garlic, minced

1 tablespoon all-purpose flour

2 cups Swanson® Chicken Broth (Regular, Natural Goodness™ **or** Certified Organic)

2 cups shredded cooked chicken

1 can (about 15 ounces) small white beans, undrained

1 can (4 ounces) chopped green chilies, drained

1 teaspoon ground cumin

1 teaspoon jalapeño hot pepper sauce

6 flour tortillas (8-inch), warmed

Shredded Monterey Jack cheese, optional

Chopped fresh cilantro, optional

START TO FINISH: 50 minutes

Prepping: 10 minutes
Cooking: 40 minutes

1. Heat the butter in a 12-inch skillet over medium heat. Add the onion and garlic powder and cook until the onion is tender. Stir in the flour and cook for 2 minutes, stirring often.

2. Stir the broth into the skillet. Cook and stir for 10 minutes or until the mixture boils and thickens.

3. Add the chicken, beans, chilies, cumin and hot sauce. Reduce the heat to low. Cook for 20 minutes, stirring occasionally.

4. Line 6 small serving bowls with tortillas. Divide the chili among the bowls. Top each serving of chili with cheese and cilantro, if desired.

Moroccan Lamb Stew

Makes 8 servings

START TO FINISH:
1 hour, 50 minutes

Prepping: 15 minutes
Cooking: 1 hour,
35 minutes

1 tablespoon olive oil

2 pounds lamb for stew, cut into 1-inch pieces

½ teaspoon ground cinnamon

¼ teaspoon ground cloves

1 medium onion, chopped (about ½ cup)

4 cups Swanson® Chicken Broth (Regular, Natural Goodness™ **or** Certified Organic)

1 cup dried lentils

2 medium potatoes, cut into cubes (about 2 cups)

Hot cooked couscous (optional)

Chopped fresh cilantro leaves (optional)

1. Heat the oil in a 4-quart saucepan over medium-high heat. Add the lamb in 2 batches and cook until it's well browned on all sides, stirring often. Remove the lamb with a slotted spoon to a medium bowl and set it aside. Sprinkle the cinnamon and cloves over the lamb and stir until it's coated.

2. Reduce the heat to medium. Add the onion to the saucepan and cook until tender-crisp.

3. Stir the broth into the saucepan. Heat to a boil. Return the lamb to the pan and reduce the heat to low. Cover and cook for 1 hour.

4. Add the lentils and potatoes. Cook for 20 minutes more or until the lentils and potatoes are tender. Stir the stew occasionally while cooking. Serve the stew over the couscous and sprinkle with the cilantro, if desired.

Thai Roasted Squash Soup

Makes 6 servings

- **2 tablespoons canola oil**
- **2 teaspoons curry powder**
- **1 butternut squash (about 2½ pounds), peeled, seeded and cut into 2-inch pieces (about 6 cups)**
- **1 large sweet onion, cut into eighths**
- **1 tablespoon chopped fresh ginger**
- **3 cups Swanson® Chicken Broth (Regular, Natural Goodness™ or Certified Organic)**
- **1 can (14 ounces) coconut milk**
- **3 tablespoons chopped fresh cilantro leaves**

1. Heat the oven to 425°F.

2. Stir the oil and curry in a large bowl. Add the squash and onions and toss to coat. Spread vegetables onto a shallow-sided baking pan.

3. Bake for 25 minutes until the vegetables are golden brown, stirring occasionally.

4. Put the vegetables and ginger in a 3-quart saucepan. Stir in the broth and cream of coconut. Heat to a boil. Reduce the heat to low. Cook for 20 minutes or until the vegetables are tender.

5. Spoon ⅓ of the soup mixture into an electric blender container. Cover and blend until smooth. Pour into saucepan. Repeat the blending process with the remaining soup mixture. Heat the soup over low heat and season to taste. Divide the soup among 6 serving bowls. Sprinkle each serving of soup with cilantro.

START TO FINISH:
1 hour

Prepping: 10 minutes
Baking/Cooking:
50 minutes

Time-Saving Tip:
Ready-cut butternut squash, sold in plastic bags, may be available in some produce sections of supermarkets.

Soups and Stews

Breakfast and Brunch

Easy Substitution Tip:
Substitute cooked chicken or turkey for the ham.

Pennsylvania Dutch Ham & Noodle Casserole

Makes 4 servings

- 1 tablespoon vegetable oil
- 2 cups cubed cooked ham (about 1 pound)
- 1 medium onion, chopped (about ½ cup)
- 1 can (10¾ ounces) Campbell's® Condensed Cream of Mushroom Soup (Regular **or** 98% Fat Free)
- 8 ounces extra-sharp Cheddar cheese, sliced
- 8 ounces extra-wide egg noodles (2 cups), cooked and drained

1. Heat the oil in a 4-quart saucepan over medium-high heat. Add the ham and onion. Cook and stir until the onion is tender.

2. Stir the soup into the saucepan. Reduce the heat to medium. Cook and stir for 5 minutes. Add the cheese and stir until the cheese melts. Gently stir in the noodles. Heat through, stirring often.

Breakfast Tacos

Makes 4 tacos

START TO FINISH:
20 minutes

Prepping: 10 minutes
Cooking: 10 minutes

Easy Substitution Tip:
Substitute crumbled
cooked pork sausage for
the bacon.

1 **tablespoon butter**
1 **cup diced cooked potato**
4 **eggs, beaten**
4 **slices bacon, cooked and crumbled**
4 **flour tortillas (6-inch), warmed**
¾ **cup shredded Cheddar cheese**
½ **cup Pace® Picante Sauce**

1. Heat the butter in a 10-inch skillet over medium heat. Add the potato and cook until it's lightly browned. Add the eggs and bacon. Cook and stir with a fork until the eggs are set but still moist.

2. Spoon **about ½ cup** of the potato mixture down the center of each tortilla. Top with the cheese and picante sauce. Fold the tortilla in half.

Apple Pecan Pastries

Makes 12 pastries

½ of a 17.3 ounce package Pepperidge Farm® Frozen Puff Pastry Sheets (1 sheet)

1 cup packed brown sugar

½ cup all-purpose flour

1 teaspoon ground cinnamon

⅛ teaspoon ground nutmeg

2 medium Granny Smith apples, peeled and diced (about 2 cups)

1 cup chopped pecans

1 tablespoon cold butter, cut into pieces

Water

Confectioners' sugar

START TO FINISH:
1 hour, 45 minutes

Thawing: 40 minutes
Prepping: 20 minutes
Baking: 15 minutes
Cooling: 30 minutes

1. Thaw the pastry sheet at room temperature for 40 minutes or until it's easy to handle. Heat the oven to 375°F. Lightly grease a baking sheet.

2. Mix the brown sugar, flour, cinnamon and nutmeg in a large bowl. Add the apples, pecans and butter and toss to coat.

3. Unfold the pastry sheet on a lightly floured surface. Roll the sheet into a 15×10-inch rectangle.

4. With the short side facing you, spoon the apple mixture on the bottom half of the pastry to within 2 inches of the edges. Brush the pastry edges with some water. Starting at the short side closest to you, roll up like a jelly roll, pressing seam gently to seal. Tuck in the ends to seal. Place the roll seam-side down on the work surface. Cut into 12 (1¼-inch) slices. Place on baking sheet 2 inches apart.

5. Bake for 15 minutes or until golden. Cool on the baking sheet on a wire rack for 30 minutes. Remove from baking sheet and cool completely on the wire rack. Sift the sugar through a sieve over the pastries before serving.

Breakfast and Brunch

Cheddar-Swiss Strata

Makes 6 servings

**START TO FINISH:
25 hours, 5 minutes**

Prepping: 15 minutes
Refrigerating:
24 hours
Baking: 40 minutes
Standing: 10 minutes

Cooking for a Crowd:
Double all ingredients.
Divide the ingredients
evenly between 2 greased
12×8×2-inch shallow
baking dishes.

Vegetable cooking spray
6   cups French **or** Italian bread, cut in cubes
1   can (10¾ ounces) Campbell's® Condensed Cheddar Cheese
     Soup
4   eggs, beaten
1   cup milk
1½ cups shredded Swiss cheese (6 ounces)

1. Spray a 12×8×2-inch shallow baking dish with cooking spray.
Put the bread in the dish.

2. Beat the soup, eggs, milk and cheese with a whisk in a medium
bowl. Pour the soup mixture over the bread. Cover and refrigerate
overnight.

3. Uncover the dish. Bake at 350°F. for 40 minutes or until a knife
inserted near the center comes out clean. Let the strata stand for
10 minutes before serving.

Cranberry Apple Bread Pudding

Makes 6 servings

Vegetable cooking spray

4 cups Pepperidge Farm® Cubed Unseasoned **or** Herb Seasoned Stuffing

¾ cup dried cranberries

4 eggs

2½ cups milk

½ cup granulated sugar

½ cup chunky sweetened applesauce

1 teaspoon vanilla extract

Brandied Butter Sauce

START TO FINISH:
1 hour, 10 minutes

Prepping: 10 minutes
Baking: 40 minutes
Standing: 20 minutes

1. Heat the oven to 350°F. Spray a 12×8×2-inch shallow baking dish with cooking spray. Place the stuffing in the prepared dish. Sprinkle the cranberries over the stuffing.

2. Beat the eggs, milk, sugar, applesauce and vanilla with a whisk in a 2-quart bowl. Pour over the stuffing mixture. Let stand for 20 minutes.

3. Bake for 40 minutes or until a knife inserted near the center comes out clean. Serve warm with *Brandied Butter Sauce*.

Brandied Butter Sauce: Heat **1 stick (½ cup) butter** in a 1-quart saucepan over medium heat until the butter melts. Add ½ **cup** packed light brown sugar. Cook and stir until the sugar dissolves and the mixture is bubbly. Remove from the heat. Whisk in **2 tablespoons** brandy. Makes 1 cup.

Make Ahead Tip:
The bread pudding and sauce can both be assembled 1 day ahead. Cover and refrigerate. Remove the pudding from refrigerator to come to room temperature while the oven preheats. To reheat the sauce, microwave in a microwavable bowl on MEDIUM for 1 minute or until hot.

Breakfast and Brunch

Crabmeat Strudel

Makes 20 appetizers

START TO FINISH:
2 hours, 15 minutes

Thawing: 40 minutes
Prepping: 30 minutes
Baking: 35 minutes
Cooling: 30 minutes

Easy Substitution Tip:
Substitute 1 can
(6 ounces) crabmeat for
the fresh crabmeat.

1 package (17.3 ounces) Pepperidge Farm® Frozen Puff Pastry Sheets (2 sheets)

1 package (8 ounces) refrigerated, pasteurized crabmeat, drained

1 tablespoon lemon juice

1 package (8 ounces) cream cheese, softened

¼ cup mayonnaise

½ cup sliced almonds

3 medium green onions, sliced (about 6 tablespoons)

2 teaspoons prepared Dijon-style mustard

1 egg

1 tablespoon water

1. Thaw the pastry sheets at room temperature for 40 minutes or until they're easy to handle. Heat the oven to 375°F. Lightly grease a baking sheet.

2. Toss the crabmeat with the lemon juice in a small bowl. Stir the cream cheese, mayonnaise, almonds, onion and mustard in a medium bowl. Gently stir in the crabmeat.

3. Unfold the pastry sheet on a lightly floured surface. Roll **1** sheet into a 16×12-inch rectangle. Put the sheet on the baking sheet. With the short side facing you, spoon **half** of the crabmeat mixture lengthwise down the center third of the rectangle. Cut 2-inch wide strips along both sides of filling cutting from filling out to the edges of the dough. Fold strips at an angle across the filling, alternating from side to side. Repeat with the remaining pastry sheet and filling.

4. Stir the egg and water with a fork in a small bowl. Brush pastry with the egg mixture. Bake for 35 minutes or until golden. Cool on the baking sheet on a wire rack for 30 minutes. Slice and serve warm.

Festive Breakfast Casserole

Makes 6 servings

  8 **ounces bulk pork sausage**

12 **slices Pepperidge Farm® White Bread, cut into cubes (about 6 cups)**

1½ **cups shredded Cheddar cheese (6 ounces)**

  1 **cup Pace® Picante Sauce or Chunky Salsa**

  4 **eggs**

  ¾ **cup milk**

START TO FINISH:
3 hours

Prepping: 15 minutes
Refrigerating: 2 hours
Baking: 45 minutes

1. Cook the sausage in a 10-inch skillet over medium-high heat until the sausage is well browned, stirring frequently to break up meat. Pour off any fat. Remove the sausage with a slotted spoon and put it in a 12×8×2-inch shallow baking dish. Top with the bread and cheese.

2. Beat the picante sauce, eggs and milk with a whisk in a medium bowl. Pour over the bread mixture. Cover and refrigerate for at least 2 hours or overnight.

3. Uncover the dish. Bake at 350°F. for 45 minutes or until a knife inserted near the center comes out clean.

Breakfast and Brunch

Huevos Rancheros

Makes 6 servings

**START TO FINISH:
25 minutes**

Prepping: 5 minutes
Cooking: 20 minutes

Make Ahead Tip:
To ease preparation,
make the soup mixture
ahead of time through
step 2. Refrigerate and
reheat when ready to
serve.

2 tablespoons butter
1 small onion, chopped (about ¼ cup)
1 tablespoon chili powder
1 clove garlic, minced
1 can (10¾ ounces) Campbell's® Condensed Tomato Soup
½ cup water
1 teaspoon chopped jalapeño pepper
6 eggs
6 corn tortillas (6-inch), warmed
¼ cup shredded Cheddar cheese

1. Heat the butter in a 12-inch skillet over medium heat. Add the onion, chili powder and garlic and cook until the onion is tender.

2. Stir the soup, water and pepper into the skillet. Heat to a boil. Reduce the heat to low.

3. Crack **1** egg into a small cup. Gently slip the egg into the soup mixture. Repeat with the remaining eggs. Cover and cook until the whites are firm.

4. Divide the tortillas among 6 serving plates. Top each tortilla with an egg, soup mixture and cheese.

Easy as Brunch!

Brunch, that combination of breakfast and lunch, is a great way to bring friends and family together. Brunch is often informal, so there's no fancy preparation, and menu-planning is a breeze.

• Think buffet: Serving is so much easier and most people are used to buffet lines in restaurants.

• Plan one main breakfast dish and one main lunch dish, plus a couple of sides, such as sausage or potatoes, for a casual at-home meal. Supplement it with toast, rolls or pastry, perhaps a fruit salad, a dessert and drinks.

• What do you have on hand? Cooked chicken, beef or ham work great in quiche and frittatas; apples, pears or peaches make delicious strudels, turnovers and bread puddings; potato or egg dishes with spinach and broccoli can be real crowd-pleasers; and add cheese to eggs, quiche and biscuits.

• Shop for convenience: Use frozen, pre-cut vegetables and cooked chicken, shredded cheeses, frozen or refrigerated pastry dough and other prepared foods.

• Do as much prep work as possible in advance. Chop onions, slice vegetables, set up the buffet and the coffeemaker, make dessert.

Creamy Spinach-Stuffed Portobellos

Makes 4 servings

- **4** large portobello mushrooms
- **1** tablespoon vegetable oil
- **1** medium onion, chopped (about ½ cup)
- **1** medium tomato, chopped (about 1 cup)
- **1** bag (6 ounces) baby spinach leaves, washed
- **1** can (10¾ ounces) Campbell's® Condensed Cream of Celery Soup (Regular **or** 98% Fat Free)
- **2** tablespoon grated Parmesan cheese
- **1** tablespoon dry bread crumbs, toasted

START TO FINISH:
30 minutes

Prepping: 10 minutes
Baking/Broiling:
 20 minutes

1. Remove the stems from the mushrooms. Set the caps topside down in a 13×9×2-inch baking pan.

2. Heat the oil in a 10-inch nonstick skillet over medium heat. Add the onion and cook until the onion is tender-crisp. Add the tomatoes and spinach and cook just until the spinach is wilted. Stir in the soup and heat through.

3. Spoon the filling into the mushroom caps.

4. Bake at 425°F. for 15 minutes or until mushrooms are hot.

5. Mix the cheese with bread crumbs in a small cup. Sprinkle over the mushrooms.

6. Heat the broiler. Broil the mushrooms with the top of the mushrooms 4 inches from the heat for about 5 minutes or until topping is golden.

Breakfast and Brunch

Picante Brunch Quiche

Makes 6 servings

**START TO FINISH:
55 minutes**

Prepping: 10 minutes
Baking: 35 minutes
Standing: 10 minutes

1 cup shredded Cheddar cheese (4 ounces)
4 slices bacon, cooked and crumbled
2 medium green onions, sliced (about 2 tablespoons)
1 (9-inch) frozen pie crust
½ cup Pace® Picante Sauce
3 eggs
½ cup half-and-half **or** milk

1. Heat the oven to 375°F.

2. Arrange the cheese, bacon and green onions in the pie crust.

3. Beat the picante sauce, eggs and half-and-half with a whisk in a medium bowl. Pour over the cheese mixture.

4. Bake for 35 minutes or until crust is golden and knife inserted near the center comes out clean. Let the quiche stand for 10 minutes before serving.

French Toast Casserole

Makes 8 servings

1 loaf (16 ounces) Pepperidge Farm® Cinnamon Swirl Bread, cut into cubes (about 8 cups)

6 eggs, beaten

3 cups milk

2 teaspoons vanilla extract

Confectioners' sugar

Maple syrup (optional)

**START TO FINISH:
2 hours, 5 minutes**

Prepping: 15 minutes
Refrigerating: 1 hour
Baking: 50 minutes

1. Lightly grease a 13×9×2-inch shallow baking dish. Put the bread in the dish.

2. Beat the eggs, milk and vanilla with a whisk in a large bowl. Pour over the bread. Cover and refrigerate for 1 hour or overnight.

3. Uncover the dish. Bake at 350°F. for 50 minutes or until golden. Sift the sugar through a sieve over the top. Serve with maple syrup, if desired.

Breakfast
and Brunch

Spinach & Feta Pie

Makes 8 servings

START TO FINISH:
1 hour, 30 minutes

Thawing: 40 minutes
Prepping: 25 minutes
Baking: 25 minutes

Time-Saving Tip:

To thaw spinach, microwave on HIGH for 3 minutes, breaking apart with a fork halfway through heating.

1 **package (17.3 ounces) Pepperidge Farm® Frozen Puff Pastry Sheets (2 sheets)**

2 **tablespoons olive oil**

2 **large onions, finely chopped (about 2 cups)**

1 **teaspoon minced garlic**

2 **packages (about 10 ounces each) frozen chopped spinach, thawed and well drained**

1 **can (10¾ ounces) Campbell's® Condensed Cream of Chicken Soup (Regular or 98% Fat Free)**

2 **eggs**

1 **teaspoon dried dill weed, crushed**

1 **package (8 ounces) feta cheese, crumbled**

1. Thaw the pastry at room temperature for 40 minutes or until they're easy to handle. Heat the oven to 375°F.

2. Heat the oil in a 10-inch skillet over medium heat. Add the onions and cook until the onions are tender. Add the garlic and cook for 1 minute. Add the spinach and cook until it's dry. Remove from the heat and let the mixture cool.

3. Beat the soup, eggs and dill weed with a whisk in a large bowl. Stir in the cheese and spinach mixture.

4. Unfold **1** pastry sheet on a lightly floured surface. Roll the sheet into a 13×9-inch rectangle. Put the pastry into a 13×9-inch baking pan. Top with spinach mixture. Roll out the remaining pastry sheet and place over the spinach mixture. Using a small knife, cut 4 slits in top of pastry.

5. Bake for 25 minutes or until golden brown.

Power Breakfast Sandwiches

Makes 2 sandwiches

¼ cup peanut butter

4 slices Pepperidge Farm® 100% Stoneground Whole Wheat Natural Whole Grain Bread

¼ cup raisins

1 medium banana, sliced

Spread peanut butter on **4** bread slices. Divide raisins and banana between **2** bread slices. Top with remaining bread slices, peanut butter-side down. Cut in half.

START TO FINISH:
5 minutes

Prepping: 5 minutes

Easy Substitution Tip:
Substitute 1 large apple, cored and sliced, for the raisins and banana.

Monte Cristo Bread Pudding

Makes 8 servings

1 tablespoon butter

8 slices Pepperidge Farm® 100% Whole Wheat Natural Whole Grain Bread, cut into quarters

6 slices deli cooked ham (about 2 ounces)

6 slices deli cooked turkey breast (about 2 ounces)

6 eggs

2 cups milk

1 cup shredded Swiss cheese (4 ounces)

Maple syrup (optional)

START TO FINISH:
40 minutes

Prepping: 10 minutes
Baking: 30 minutes

Breakfast and Brunch

1. Coat the bottom of 13×9×2-inch shallow baking dish with the butter. Arrange **half** of the bread pieces on the bottom of the dish.

2. Layer the ham and turkey over the bread. Top with remaining bread pieces.

3. Beat the eggs and milk with a whisk in a medium bowl. Pour over the bread. Sprinkle with the cheese.

4. Bake at 350°F. for 30 minutes or until center is set and top is golden. Serve warm with maple syrup, if desired.

Potato Buttermilk Biscuits & Sausage Gravy

Makes 12 servings

START TO FINISH:
50 minutes

Prepping: 35 minutes
Baking/Cooking:
15 minutes

Make Ahead Tip:
The biscuits can be made 1 day ahead and stored in a plastic bag in the refrigerator. To reheat, place on a baking sheet and bake at 425°F. oven for 5 to 7 minutes.

1⅓ cups instant mashed potatoes (dry flakes)
1⅓ cups water
½ cup milk
6 tablespoons butter
2 cups all-purpose flour
1 tablespoon baking powder
1 teaspoon baking soda
¾ cup buttermilk
½ of a 16 ounce package bulk pork sausage
2 cans (10½ ounces **each**) Campbell's® Turkey Gravy
1 tablespoon chopped fresh parsley **or** 1 teaspoon dried parsley flakes, crushed

1. Prepare the potatoes using the water, milk and **2 tablespoons** butter according to the package directions, omitting the salt. Let cool.

2. Heat the oven to 425°F. Stir together the flour, baking powder and baking soda. With a pastry blender, cut in the remaining butter until the mixture resembles coarse crumbs. Stir in the potatoes and buttermilk with fork to form a soft dough. Turn out dough onto a floured surface.

3. With floured hands, gently knead the dough 4 times and pat it into a ¾-inch thick disc. Cut the dough with a 2½-inch round biscuit cutter and place the biscuits 1-inch apart on a greased baking sheet.

4. Bake for 15 minutes or until golden.

5. While the biscuits are baking, cook the sausage in a 12-inch skillet over medium-high heat until it's well browned, stirring to break up meat. Pour off the fat.

6. Stir the gravy and parsley into the skillet. Reduce the heat to low and cook until the mixture is hot and bubbling. Serve with the biscuits.

Spinach and Mushroom Frittata

Makes 8 servings

Vegetable cooking spray
10 eggs
1 can (10¾ ounces) Campbell's® Condensed Cream of Mushroom Soup (Regular or 98% Fat Free)
1 package (10 ounces) frozen chopped spinach, thawed and well drained
1½ cups shredded Swiss or Jarlsberg cheese (6 ounces)
½ teaspoon ground black pepper

1. Heat the oven to 375°F. Spray a 12×8×2-inch baking dish with cooking spray and set it aside.

2. Beat the eggs with a whisk in a large bowl. Stir in the soup. Stir in the spinach, **1 cup** of the cheese and black pepper. Pour the mixture into the prepared dish.

3. Bake for 35 minutes or until the eggs are set in the center. Sprinkle with remaining cheese. Serve immediately or cool slightly.

**START TO FINISH:
45 minutes**

Prepping: 10 minutes
Baking: 35 minutes

Make Ahead Tip:
Bake the frittata the day before. Cover and refrigerate. Remove the frittata from the refrigerator and let it stand at room temperature for about 30 minutes. Reheat in a 350°F. oven for about 20 minutes.

Breakfast and Brunch

Sandwiches and Wraps

START TO FINISH:
25 minutes

Prepping: 5 minutes
Cooking: 20 minutes

Time-Saving Tip:
Shape the burgers a day ahead, cover and refrigerate to make mealtime quicker. Or, purchase burgers already shaped at your local meat counter.

French Onion Burgers

Makes 4 burgers

- 1 **pound ground beef**
- 1 **can (10½ ounces) Campbell's® Condensed French Onion Soup**
- 4 **slices cheese**
- 4 **round hard rolls, split**

1. Shape the beef into 4 (½-inch) thick burgers.

2. Heat a 10-inch skillet over medium-high heat. Add the burgers and cook until they're well browned on both sides. Remove the burgers and set aside. Pour off any fat.

3. Stir the soup into the skillet. Heat to a boil. Return the burgers to the skillet and reduce the heat to low. Cover and cook for 5 minutes or until the burgers are cooked through*. Top with cheese and continue cooking until the cheese melts. Serve burgers in rolls with soup mixture for dipping.

The internal temperature of the burgers should reach 160°F.

Shredded BBQ Chicken Sandwiches

Makes 8 sandwiches

START TO FINISH:
30 minutes

Prepping: 10 minutes
Cooking: 20 minutes

2 jars (16 ounces each) Pace® Chunky Salsa
1 tablespoon apple cider vinegar
¼ cup packed brown sugar
½ teaspoon garlic powder
¼ teaspoon chili powder
4 skinless, boneless chicken breast halves
1 package (13 ounces) Pepperidge Farm® Sandwich Buns
  Shredded Cheddar cheese

1. Stir the salsa, vinegar, brown sugar, garlic powder and chili powder in a 2-quart saucepan over medium-high heat to a boil.

2. Add the chicken to the saucepan and reduce the heat to low. Cover and cook for 20 minutes or until chicken is cooked through*.

3. Remove the chicken from the saucepan to a cutting board. Using 2 forks, shred the chicken. Return the shredded chicken to the saucepan. Heat the chicken mixture over medium-low heat until the mixture is hot and bubbling.

4. Divide the chicken mixture among the buns and top with the cheese.

The internal temperature of the chicken should reach 160°F.

Salsa BBQ Chicken Lettuce Wraps

Makes 4 sandwiches

1¼ cups Pace® Chipotle Chunky Salsa

4 skinless, boneless chicken breast halves

4 large romaine **or** iceberg lettuce leaves

2 medium carrots, shredded (about 1 cup)

2 stalks celery, sliced (about ½ cup)

¼ cup crumbled blue cheese (about 1 ounce)

START TO FINISH:
1 hour, 30 minutes

Prepping/Grilling:
30 minutes
Marinating: 1 hour

1. Pour ½ **cup** of the salsa into a 2-quart shallow, nonmetallic dish or gallon-size resealable plastic bag. Add the chicken and turn it over to coat with the salsa. Cover the dish or seal the bag and refrigerate for 1 hour, turning the chicken over a few times while it's marinating.

2. Lightly oil the grill rack and heat the grill to medium. Remove the chicken from marinade. Throw away any remaining marinade.

3. Grill the chicken for 10 minutes or until the chicken is cooked through*, turning the chicken over halfway through cooking and brushing it often with ¼ **cup** of the remaining salsa. Remove the chicken from grill and put on a cutting board. Let stand for 5 minutes. Thinly slice the chicken breasts.

4. Put lettuce leaves on the work surface. Arrange ¼ of the sliced chicken down the center of each lettuce leaf. Top the each serving of chicken with ¼ **cup** carrots, **2 tablespoons** celery, **2 tablespoons** of the remaining salsa and **1 tablespoon** cheese. Roll up each lettuce leaf to enclose the filling. Serve immediately.

The internal temperature of the chicken should reach 160°F.

Sandwiches
and Wraps

Zesty Chicken Mozzarella Sandwiches

Makes 4 sandwiches

START TO FINISH:
45 minutes

Prepping: 10 minutes
Marinating:
   10 minutes
Baking/Grilling:
   25 minutes

⅓ cup prepared Italian salad dressing

4 skinless, boneless chicken breast halves

1 loaf (11.75 ounces) Pepperidge Farm® Frozen Mozzarella Garlic Cheese Bread

1 medium red onion, sliced (about ½ cup)

1. Pour the dressing in a nonmetallic shallow dish. Add the chicken and turn it to coat with the marinade. Cover and refrigerate for 10 minutes.

2. Heat the oven to 400°F.

3. Remove the bread from the bag. Place the frozen bread halves, cut-side up, on an ungreased baking sheet. (If bread halves are frozen together, carefully insert fork between the halves to separate.)

4. Place the baking sheet on middle oven rack. Bake for 10 minutes or until it's hot.

5. Lightly oil the grill rack and heat the grill to medium. Remove the chicken from the marinade. Throw away any remaining marinade.

6. Grill the chicken for 15 minutes or until the chicken is cooked through*, turning the chicken halfway through cooking.

7. Place the chicken and red onion on the bottom bread half. Top with the remaining bread half. Cut the bread into quarters so each serving has 1 chicken breast.

The internal temperature of the chicken should reach 160°F.

Chicken & Black Bean Quesadillas

Makes 10 quesadillas

1 can (10¾ ounces) Campbell's® Condensed Cheddar Cheese Soup

½ cup Pace® Chunky Salsa **or** Picante Sauce

1 cup canned black beans, rinsed and drained

2 cans (4.5 ounces **each**) Swanson® Premium Chunk Chicken Breast, drained

10 flour tortillas (8-inch)
   Fiesta Rice

START TO FINISH:
20 minutes

Prepping: 5 minutes
Cooking/Baking:
15 minutes

1. Stir the soup, salsa, beans and chicken in a 1½-quart saucepan. Cook and stir over medium heat until hot.

2. Put the tortillas on 2 baking sheets. Top half of each tortilla with about ⅓ **cup** of the soup mixture, spreading to within ½-inch of the edge. Moisten the edge of each tortilla with water. Fold over and press the edges together to seal.

3. Bake at 425°F. for 5 minutes or until the filling is hot. Serve with *Fiesta Rice*.

Fiesta Rice: Heat **1 can** (10½ ounces) Campbell's® Condensed Chicken Broth, ½ **cup** water and ½ **cup** Pace® Chunky Salsa in a 1½-quart saucepan over high heat to a boil. Stir in **2 cups uncooked** instant white rice. Cover and remove from the heat. Let stand for 5 minutes, and then fluff the rice with a fork.

Sandwiches and Wraps

Chicken Salsa Pockets

Makes 6 sandwiches

START TO FINISH:
15 minutes

Prepping/Cooking:
15 minutes

Easy Substitution Tip:
Substitute 2 cans
(4.5 ounces each)
Swanson® Premium
Chunk Chicken breast,
drained, for the cooked
chicken.

1 can (10¾ ounces) Campbell's® Condensed Cream
    of Chicken Soup (Regular **or** 98% Fat Free)
½ cup Pace® Chunky Salsa
2 cups cooked chicken, cut into strips
½ cup shredded Cheddar cheese
3 pita breads (6-inch), cut in half, forming 2 pockets
    Green leaf lettuce leaves

1. Stir the soup, salsa and chicken in a 2-quart saucepan. Cook and stir over medium heat until hot. Stir in the cheese. Cook until the cheese melts.

2. Line the pita halves with lettuce. Spoon about ⅓ **cup** chicken mixture into each pita half.

Fontina Turkey Panini

Makes 2 sandwiches

4 slices Pepperidge Farm® Farmhouse™ Sourdough Bread

2 tablespoons honey mustard salad dressing

4 slices fontina cheese (about 4 ounces)

2 slices smoked turkey (about 2 ounces)

4 bread-and-butter pickle sandwich slices

Olive oil

START TO FINISH:
15 minutes

Prepping/Cooking:
15 minutes

1. Put **2** bread slices on a work surface. Spread each with **1 tablespoon** salad dressing. Top each with **2** slices cheese, **1** slice turkey, **2** pickle slices and remaining bread slices.

2. Brush the tops of the sandwiches with some olive oil. Heat a grill pan or skillet over medium heat. Put the sandwiches oil-side down on pan. Cook for 2 minutes or until sandwich is lightly browned. Brush the tops of the sandwiches with some olive oil.

3. Turn the sandwiches over and cook for 2 minutes or until lightly browned and cheese melts, pressing with a spatula occasionally.

Sandwiches and Wraps

Peanut Butter Banana Tacos

Makes 4 sandwiches

START TO FINISH:
10 minutes

Prepping: 10 minutes

Easy Substitution Tip:
Substitute cream cheese or your favorite jelly for the peanut butter.

4 tablespoons crunchy peanut butter

4 slices Pepperidge Farm® Cinnamon Swirl **or** Cinnamon Raisin Swirl Bread

1 medium ripe banana

1. Spread the peanut butter on the bread slices.

2. Cut the banana into crosswise halves. Cut each **half** into 2 lengthwise pieces. Place **1** banana piece on each bread slice and roll up.

Balsamic Berry and Turkey Salad Sandwiches

Makes 2 sandwiches

START TO FINISH:
40 minutes

Prepping: 10 minutes
Refrigerating:
  30 minutes

Easy Substitution Tip:
Substitute Pepperidge Farm® Honey Whole Wheat Whole Grain Bread for the Honey Oat Whole Grain Bread.

1 tablespoon balsamic vinegar

2 tablespoons mayonnaise

4 ounces skinless deli turkey breast, chopped

½ cup chopped fresh strawberries

¼ cup sliced green onions

2 tablespoons chopped pecans

4 slices Pepperidge Farm® Honey Oat Whole Grain Bread, toasted

Green leaf lettuce leaves

1. Beat the vinegar and mayonnaise with a fork in a medium bowl. Stir in the turkey, strawberries, green onions and pecans. Cover and refrigerate for 30 minutes.

2. Divide the turkey mixture between **2** bread slices. Top with lettuce and remaining bread slices.

Southwestern Chicken & Pepper Wraps

Makes 4 sandwiches

2 tablespoons vegetable oil

1 pound boneless chicken breasts, cut into strips

1 medium red pepper, cut into 2-inch-long strips
(about 1½ cups)

1 medium green pepper, cut into 2-inch-long strips
(about 1½ cups)

1 small onion, sliced (about ¼ cup)

1 can (10¾ ounces) Campbell's® Condensed Golden
Mushroom Soup

1 cup water

1 cup canned black beans, rinsed and drained (optional)

1 cup **uncooked** instant white rice

8 flour tortillas (8-inch), warmed

START TO FINISH:
35 minutes

Prepping: 10 minutes
Cooking: 20 minutes
Standing: 5 minutes

1. Heat **1 tablespoon** oil in a 10-inch skillet over medium-high heat. Add the chicken and cook until it's well browned, stirring often. Remove the chicken with a slotted spoon and set aside.

2. Reduce the heat to medium. Add the remaining oil. Add the peppers and onions and cook until tender-crisp.

3. Stir the soup, water and beans into the skillet. Heat to a boil. Reduce the heat to low. Return the chicken to the skillet and cover. Cook for 5 minutes.

4. Stir in the rice. Cover the skillet and remove from the heat. Let stand for 5 minutes or until the chicken is cooked through*. Fluff the rice with a fork.

5. Spoon **about ¾ cup** chicken mixture down the center of each tortilla. Fold the tortilla around the filling.

*The internal temperature of the chicken should reach 160°F.

Grilled Vegetable Sandwiches

Makes 4 sandwiches

**START TO FINISH:
25 minutes**

Prepping: 10 minutes
Grilling: 15 minutes

Time-Saving Tip:

Place the rolls cut-side down on the grill to toast while the vegetables are grilling.

½ cup Pace® Picante Sauce
¼ cup red wine vinegar
1 teaspoon dried oregano leaves, crushed
¼ teaspoon garlic powder **or** 2 cloves garlic, minced
2 portobello mushrooms
1 small eggplant, sliced lengthwise ½-inch thick
2 small zucchini, sliced lengthwise
1 large green **or** red pepper, cut into halves
4 long sandwich rolls (8-inches), split and toasted
½ cup shredded mozzarella cheese

1. Stir the picante sauce, vinegar, oregano and garlic in a small bowl and set aside.

2. Lightly oil the grill rack and heat the grill to medium. Grill the mushrooms, eggplant, zucchini and pepper for 15 minutes or until the vegetables are tender, turning halfway through cooking and brushing them often with the picante sauce mixture while they're grilling. Slice the mushrooms and pepper.

3. Divide the vegetables among the rolls and top with cheese. Serve with additional picante sauce.

Open-Faced Garden Frittata Sandwiches

Makes 2 sandwiches

Vegetable cooking spray
¼ cup shredded zucchini
¼ cup chopped red pepper
1 cup cholesterol-free egg substitute
¼ cup crumbled goat cheese
1 tablespoon chopped fresh chives
Freshly ground black pepper
4 slices Pepperidge Farm® 9 Grain Natural Whole Grain Bread, toasted

START TO FINISH:
15 minutes

Prepping: 5 minutes
Cooking: 10 minutes

Easy Substitution Tip:
Substitute Pepperidge Farm® 15 Grain Natural Whole Grain Bread for the 9 Grain Natural Whole Grain Bread.

1. Spray a 10-inch nonstick skillet with cooking spray and heat over medium heat 1 minute. Add the zucchini and red pepper. Cover and cook until tender. Remove vegetables. Wipe the skillet with a paper towel.

2. Spray skillet with cooking spray and heat over medium heat 1 minute. Add the egg substitute and top with cooked vegetables, goat cheese and chives. Reduce the heat to medium-low. Cook for 5 minutes or until the eggs are set but still moist. Season to taste with black pepper. Remove the frittata from the skillet and cut it into quarters. Top each bread slice with a frittata wedge.

Sandwiches and Wraps

Sausage & Pepper Heros

Makes 12 sandwiches

START TO FINISH:
1 hour, 40 minutes

Prepping: 10 minutes
Baking: 1 hour,
30 minutes

3 pounds sweet **or** hot Italian pork sausage, cut into 2-inch pieces
1 jar (67 ounces) Prego® Traditional Italian Sauce (7½ cups)
3 medium green peppers, cut into 2-inch-long strips (about 4½ cups)
3 medium onions, sliced (about 1½ cups)
12 long sandwich rolls (8-inches), split
   Grated Parmesan cheese

1. Put the sausage in a 16½×12×2 ½-inch disposable foil pan.

2. Bake at 425°F. for 45 minutes or until the sausage is browned. Carefully pour off juices that are in the pan.

3. Stir in the Italian sauce, peppers and onions. Cover the pan with foil.

4. Bake for 45 minutes more or until the sausage reaches an internal temperature of 160°F.

5. Divide the sausage and peppers among the roll halves. Top with the cheese and remaining roll halves.

Soup and Sandwich Combos

Campbell's® Soup	Sandwich
Tomato	Grilled cheese
Chicken Noodle	Ham & cheese pita pockets
Chili Beef	Grilled pepper jack cheese sandwiches
Bean with Bacon	Corned beef on rye bread
New England Clam Chowder	Tuna melt on English muffin
Cream of Mushroom	Grilled hamburger topped with tomato and lettuce
Cream of Broccoli	Tuna salad on sandwich roll with tomatoes
Broccoli Cheese	Chicken salad on whole wheat with lettuce
Minestrone	Cheesesteak with fried onions
French Onion	Hot roast beef on French bread
Split Pea & Ham	Corned beef with coleslaw on rye
Beef Vegetable Barley	Turkey submarine with lettuce, tomato, and onion
Chicken NoodleO's	Mini cheese pizzas
Chicken with Wild Rice	Turkey with mozzarella & roasted red pepper on crusty roll
Fiesta Nacho Cheese	Roast beef wrap
Creamy Chicken Noodle	Grilled vegetable sandwich on focaccia
Vegetable Beef	Smoked turkey with Swiss on marbled rye
Beef Noodle	Roasted pepper and mozzarella cheese wrap

Pizza Turnovers

Makes 8 turnovers

1 package (17.3 ounces) Pepperidge Farm® Frozen Puff Pastry Sheets (2 sheets)

1 egg

1 tablespoon water

2 cups Prego® Chunky Garden Mushroom Supreme **or** Mushroom & Green Pepper Italian Sauce

2 cups shredded mozzarella cheese (8 ounces)

1 cup chopped pepperoni

START TO FINISH:
1 hour, 40 minutes

Thawing: 40 minutes
Prepping: 35 minutes
Baking: 25 minutes

1. Thaw the pastry sheets at room temperature for 40 minutes or until they're easy to handle. Heat the oven to 400°F. Lightly grease 2 baking sheets. Stir the egg and water with a fork in a small bowl.

2. Stir the Italian sauce, cheese and pepperoni in a medium bowl.

3. Unfold **1** pastry sheet on a lightly floured surface. Roll the sheet into a 12-inch square. Cut the pastry into 4 (6-inch) squares. Repeat with the remaining pastry sheet.

4. Spoon about ½ **cup** pepperoni mixture onto the center of each square. Brush the pastry edges with the egg mixture. Fold the pastry over the filling to form a triangle and then crimp the edges to seal. Place the turnovers on 2 baking sheets. Brush the turnovers with the egg mixture.

5. Bake for 25 minutes or until golden. Remove the turnovers from the baking sheets and cool slightly on wire rack. Serve warm.

Sandwiches and Wraps

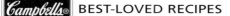

Tuna Niçoise Sandwiches

Makes 2 sandwiches

START TO FINISH:
10 minutes

Prepping: 10 minutes

Easy Substitution Tip:
Substitute Pepperidge
Farm® 100% Whole
Wheat Natural Whole
Grain Bread for the
Multi-Grain Natural
Whole Grain Bread.

2 tablespoons mayonnaise

2 tablespoons Dijon-style mustard

1 can (6 ounces) chunk white tuna packed in water, drained
and flaked

2 tablespoons sliced green onion

1 tablespoon pitted, chopped kalamata olives

1 tablespoon drained capers

4 slices Pepperidge Farm® Multi-Grain Natural Whole Grain
Bread

Red leaf lettuce leaves

1. Stir mayonnaise and mustard in a small bowl. Stir in the tuna,
green onion, olives and capers.

2. Top **2** bread slices with lettuce. Divide the tuna mixture between
the bread slices. Top with the remaining bread slices.

Philadelphia Cheese Steaks

Makes 4 sandwiches

2 tablespoons vegetable oil

1 large onion, sliced (about 1 cup)

1 large red **or** green pepper, thinly sliced (about 1½ cups)

1 cup sliced mushrooms

4 frozen beef sandwich steaks (about 2 ounces **each**)

1 can (10¾ ounces) Campbell's® Condensed Cheddar Cheese Soup

4 long sandwich rolls (8-inches), split

START TO FINISH:
20 minutes

Prepping: 10 minutes
Cooking: 10 minutes

1. Heat the oil in a 12-inch skillet over medium-high heat. Add the onion, pepper and mushrooms in 2 batches and cook until tender. Remove the vegetables with a slotted spoon.

2. Add the steaks to the skillet. Cook and stir until the steaks are no longer pink.

3. Spoon the soup into a microwavable bowl. Cover and microwave on HIGH for 1½ to 2 minutes or until hot. Let stand for 1 minute, then stir.

4. Spread **2 tablespoons** soup mixture over the cut sides of each roll. Divide the steak and vegetables among the rolls and top with remaining soup.

Sandwiches and Wraps

Poultry

START TO FINISH:
20 minutes

Prepping/Cooking:
20 minutes

Tasty 2-Step Chicken

Makes 6 servings

- 1 tablespoon vegetable oil
- 4 to 6 skinless, boneless chicken breast halves
- 1 can (10¾ ounces) Campbell's® Condensed Cream of Mushroom Soup (Regular **or** 98% Fat Free)
- ½ cup water

1. Heat the oil in a 10-inch skillet over medium-high heat. Add the chicken and cook for 10 minutes or until it's browned. Set the chicken aside. Pour off any fat.

2. Stir the soup and water into the skillet. Heat to a boil. Return the chicken to the skillet and reduce the heat to low. Cover and cook for 5 minutes or until the chicken is cooked through*.

The internal temperature of the chicken should reach 160°F.

Cranberry Chicken

Makes 6 servings

START TO FINISH:
25 minutes

Prepping: 5 minutes
Cooking: 20 minutes

1 tablespoon vegetable oil

4 to 6 skinless, boneless chicken breast halves

1 can (10¾ ounces) Campbell's® Condensed Cream of Mushroom Soup (Regular **or** 98% Fat Free)

¼ cup cranberry juice

¼ cup orange juice

1 tablespoon dried cranberries

1 tablespoon chopped fresh sage leaves **or** 1 teaspoon dried sage leaves, crushed

⅛ teaspoon ground black pepper

Hot cooked rice

Sliced green onions

1. Heat the oil in a 10-inch skillet over medium-high heat. Add the chicken and cook for 10 minutes or until it's well browned on both sides. Remove the chicken and set aside.

2. Stir the soup, cranberry juice, orange juice, cranberries, sage and black pepper into the skillet. Heat to a boil. Return the chicken to the skillet and reduce the heat to low. Cover and cook for 5 minutes or until the chicken is cooked through*. Serve with the rice and sprinkle with the green onions.

The internal temperature of the chicken should reach 160°F.

Asian Chicken with Peanuts

Makes 4 servings

2 tablespoons cornstarch

1¾ cups Swanson® Chicken Broth (Regular, Natural Goodness™ **or** Certified Organic)

2 tablespoons soy sauce

½ teaspoon ground ginger

½ teaspoon sesame oil (optional)

2 tablespoons vegetable oil

1 pound skinless, boneless chicken breasts, cut into strips

2 cups broccoli flowerets

1 large red pepper, cut into 2-inch-long strips (about 2 cups)

2 cloves garlic, minced

½ cup salted peanuts

Hot cooked rice

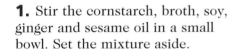

**START TO FINISH:
30 minutes**

Prepping: 15 minutes
Cooking: 15 minutes

1. Stir the cornstarch, broth, soy, ginger and sesame oil in a small bowl. Set the mixture aside.

2. Heat **1 tablespoon** of the oil in a 12-inch skillet over medium-high heat. Add the chicken and stir-fry until it's well browned. Remove the chicken with a slotted spoon and set aside.

3. Reduce the heat to medium and add the remaining oil. Add the broccoli, pepper and garlic. Stir-fry until the broccoli is tender-crisp.

4. Stir the cornstarch mixture and stir it into the skillet. Cook and stir until the mixture boils and thickens. Return the chicken to the skillet. Add the peanuts and cook until the mixture is hot and bubbling. Serve over the rice.

Chicken & Roasted Garlic Risotto

Makes 6 servings

START TO FINISH:
25 minutes

Prepping/Cooking:
   20 minutes
Standing: 5 minutes

Easy Substitution Tip:
For flavor variation, use 1 cup frozen peas and pearl onions or frozen mixed vegetables for the 1 cup frozen peas and carrots.

4 to 6 skinless, boneless chicken breast halves

1 tablespoon butter

1 can (10¾ ounces) Campbell's® Condensed Cream of Chicken Soup (Regular **or** 98% Fat Free)

1 can (10¾ ounces) Campbell's® Condensed Cream of Mushroom with Roasted Garlic Soup

2 cups water

2 cups **uncooked** instant white rice

1 cup frozen peas and carrots

1. Season chicken as desired.

2. Heat the butter in a 10-inch skillet over medium-high heat. Add the chicken and cook for 10 minutes or until it's well browned on both sides. Remove the chicken and set aside.

3. Stir the soups and water into the skillet. Heat to a boil. Stir in the rice and vegetables. Return the chicken to the skillet and reduce the heat to low. Cover and cook for 5 minutes or until the chicken is cooked through*. Remove the skillet from the heat. Let stand for 5 minutes.

The internal temperature of the chicken should reach 160°F.

Cheesy Chicken Quesadillas

Makes 4 servings

1 **pound skinless, boneless chicken breasts, cut into cubes**

1 **can (10¾ ounces) Campbell's® Condensed Southwest Style Pepper Jack Soup**

¼ **cup water**

8 **flour tortillas (8-inch), warmed**

Pace® Chunky Salsa

START TO FINISH: 25 minutes

Prepping: 5 minutes
Cooking/Baking:
   20 minutes

1. Heat the oven to 425°F.

2. Cook the chicken in a 10-inch nonstick skillet over medium-high heat for 5 minutes or until it's well browned, stirring often.

3. Stir the soup and water into the skillet. Heat to a boil. Cover and cook for 5 minutes or until the chicken is cooked through*.

4. Put the tortillas on 2 baking sheets. Top **half** of each tortilla with ⅓ **cup** soup mixture, spreading to within ½-inch of the edge. Moisten the edge of each tortilla with water. Fold over and press the edges together to seal.

5. Bake for 5 minutes or until the filling is hot. Cut into wedges and serve with the salsa.

The internal temperature of the chicken should reach 160°F.

Chicken Creole with Chile Cream Sauce

Makes 6 servings

START TO FINISH:
20 minutes

Prepping/Cooking:
20 minutes

4 to 6 skinless, boneless chicken breast halves

2 teaspoons Creole **or** Cajun seasoning

1 tablespoon olive oil

1 can (10¾ ounces) Campbell's® Condensed Cream of Chicken Soup (Regular **or** 98% Fat Free)

½ cup water

1 can (4 ounces) chopped green chiles

1 teaspoon lime juice

¼ cup sour cream

Hot cooked rice

1. Season the chicken with the Creole seasoning.

2. Heat the oil in a 10-inch skillet over medium-high heat. Add the chicken and cook for 10 minutes or until it's well browned on both sides. Remove the chicken and set aside.

3. Stir the soup, water, chiles and lime juice into the skillet. Heat to a boil. Return the chicken to the skillet and reduce the heat to low. Cover and cook for 5 minutes or until the chicken is cooked through*.

4. Stir the sour cream into the skillet and heat through. Serve with the rice.

The internal temperature of the chicken should reach 160°F.

Chicken Scampi

Makes 6 servings

2 tablespoons butter

4 to 6 skinless, boneless chicken breast halves

1 can (10¾ ounces) Campbell's® Condensed Cream of Chicken Soup (Regular **or** 98% Fat Free)

¼ cup water

2 teaspoons lemon juice

2 cloves garlic, minced **or** ½ teaspoon garlic powder

Hot cooked pasta

START TO FINISH:
25 minutes

Prepping: 5 minutes
Cooking: 20 minutes

1. Heat the butter in a 10-inch skillet over medium-high heat. Add the chicken and cook for 10 minutes or until it's well browned on both sides. Remove the chicken and set aside.

2. Stir the soup, water, lemon juice and garlic into the skillet. Heat to a boil. Return the chicken to the skillet and reduce the heat to low. Cover and cook for 5 minutes or until the chicken is cooked through*. Serve with the pasta.

The internal temperature of the chicken should reach 160°F.

Country Chicken with Couscous

Makes 8 servings

START TO FINISH:
1 hour, 20 minutes

Prepping: 10 minutes
Cooking: 1 hour, 10 minutes

Make Ahead Tip:
Prepare the recipe. Cover and refrigerate overnight. Heat in saucepot over low heat for 15 minutes or until mixture is heated through, stirring often.

2 tablespoons olive **or** vegetable oil
5 to 6 pounds chicken parts
2 jars (14 ounces **each**) Prego® Traditional Italian Sauce
½ cup dry Marsala
¾ pound fresh mushrooms, sliced (about 4 cups)
1 large onion, chopped (about 1 cup)
½ cup chopped fresh parsley
2 cans (2.25 ounces **each**) sliced pitted ripe olives, drained
¼ cup drained capers
   Hot cooked couscous

1. Heat the oil in a 6-quart saucepot over medium-high heat. Add the chicken in 2 batches and cook for 10 minutes or until it's well browned on all sides. Remove chicken and set aside. Pour off any fat.

2. Stir the Italian sauce, Marsala, mushrooms, onion, parsley, olives and capers into the saucepot. Heat to a boil. Return the chicken to the saucepot and reduce the heat to low. Cover and cook for 30 minutes, stirring occasionally.

3. Uncover the saucepot. Cook for 15 minutes more or until the chicken is cooked through*. Serve with the couscous.

The internal temperature of the chicken should reach 170°F.

Creamy Enchiladas Verde

Makes 4 servings

1 can (10¾ ounces) Campbell's® Condensed Creamy Chicken
   Verde Soup
½ teaspoon garlic powder
1½ cups chopped cooked chicken
⅔ cup shredded Cheddar **or** Monterey Jack cheese
8 corn tortillas (6-inch), warmed
¼ cup milk

START TO FINISH:
30 minutes

Prepping: 10 minutes
Baking: 20 minutes

1. Stir ½ **can** of the soup, garlic powder, chicken, and ⅓ **cup** of the cheese in a medium bowl.

2. Spoon **about** ⅓ **cup** of the chicken mixture down the center of each tortilla. Roll up the tortillas and place them seam-side down in a 12×8×2-inch shallow baking dish.

3. Stir the remaining soup and milk in a small bowl. Pour the soup mixture over the filled tortillas. Top with the remaining cheese.

4. Bake at 375°F. for 20 minutes or until the enchiladas are hot and bubbly.

Poultry

Chicken Dijon with Noodles

Makes 6 servings

START TO FINISH:
25 minutes

Prepping/Cooking:
25 minutes

Leftover Tip:
Cut up leftover chicken and add back to leftover sauce. Cover and refrigerate. Reheat chicken mixture and serve over toast topped with some chopped apple.

2 tablespoons butter
4 to 6 skinless, boneless chicken breast halves
1 medium onion, chopped (about ½ cup)
1 can (10¾ ounces) Campbell's® Condensed Cream of Mushroom Soup (Regular **or** 98% Fat Free)
¼ cup apple juice **or** milk
1 tablespoon Dijon-style mustard
1 tablespoon chopped fresh parsley **or** 1 teaspoon dried parsley flakes
Hot cooked noodles

1. Heat the butter in a 10-inch skillet over medium-high heat. Add the chicken and cook for 10 minutes or until it's well browned on both sides. Remove the chicken and set aside.

2. Reduce the heat to medium. Add the onion and cook until tender.

3. Stir the soup, apple juice, mustard and parsley into the skillet. Heat to a boil. Return the chicken to the skillet and reduce the heat to low. Cover and cook for 5 minutes or until the chicken is cooked through*. Serve with the noodles.

The internal temperature of the chicken should reach 160°F.

Paprika Chicken with Sour Cream Gravy

Makes 6 servings

- ½ cup all-purpose flour
- 2 teaspoons paprika
- 1 teaspoon **each** garlic powder, ground black pepper **and** ground red pepper
- 4 to 6 skinless, boneless chicken breast halves
- 4 tablespoons butter
- 1 can (10¾ ounces) Campbell's® Condensed Cream of Chicken Soup (Regular **or** 98% Fat Free)
- 2 medium green onions, sliced (about ¼ cup)
- 1 container (8 ounces) sour cream

START TO FINISH:
25 minutes

Prepping: 5 minutes
Cooking: 20 minutes

1. Mix the flour, paprika, garlic powder, black pepper and red pepper on a plate. Coat the chicken with the flour mixture.

2. Heat the butter in a 10-inch skillet over medium heat. Add the chicken and cook for 10 minutes or until it's well browned on both sides. Remove the chicken and set aside.

3. Stir the soup and green onions into the skillet. Heat to a boil. Return the chicken to the skillet and reduce the heat to low. Cover and cook for 5 minutes or until the chicken is cooked through*. Stir in the sour cream.

*The internal temperature of the chicken should reach 160°F.

Poultry

Lemon Broccoli Chicken

Makes 6 servings

START TO FINISH:
25 minutes

Prepping: 5 minutes
Cooking: 20 minutes

Easy Substitution Tip:
Add whole grains to
your diet by serving
cooked barley, whole
wheat pasta or brown
rice instead of regular
rice.

1 lemon

1 tablespoon vegetable oil

4 to 6 skinless, boneless chicken breast halves

1 can (10¾ ounces) Campbell's® Condensed Cream of Broccoli
   Soup (Regular **or** 98% Fat Free)

½ cup milk

⅛ teaspoon ground black pepper

Hot cooked rice

1. Cut **4** thin slices of the lemon. Squeeze **2 teaspoons** of juice from
the remaining lemon.

2. Heat the oil in a 10-inch skillet over medium-high heat. Add the
chicken and cook for 10 minutes or until it's well browned on both
sides. Remove the chicken and set aside.

3. Stir the soup, milk, lemon juice and black pepper into the skillet.
Heat to a boil. Return the chicken to the skillet and reduce the heat to
low. Top the chicken with the lemon slices. Cover and cook for
5 minutes or until the chicken is cooked through*. Serve with the rice.

The internal temperature of the chicken should reach 160°F.

Skillet Chicken Parmesan

Makes 6 servings

¼ cup grated Parmesan cheese

1½ cups Prego® Traditional Italian Sauce **or** Prego® Organic Tomato & Basil Italian Sauce

1 tablespoon olive oil

4 to 6 skinless, boneless chicken breast halves

1½ cups shredded part-skim mozzarella cheese (6 ounces)

START TO FINISH:
35 minutes

Prepping: 5 minutes
Cooking: 25 minutes
Standing: 5 minutes

1. Stir **3 tablespoons** Parmesan cheese into the Italian sauce.

2. Heat the oil in a 12-inch skillet over medium-high heat. Add the chicken and cook for 10 minutes or until it's well browned on both sides.

3. Pour the sauce mixture into the skillet. Turn the chicken to coat with sauce. Reduce the heat to medium. Cover and cook for 10 minutes or until the chicken is cooked through*.

4. Sprinkle the mozzarella cheese and the remaining Parmesan cheese over the chicken. Let stand for 5 minutes or until the cheese melts.

The internal temperature of the chicken should reach 160°F.

Savory Orange Chicken with Sage

Makes 6 servings

START TO FINISH:
30 minutes

Prepping: 10 minutes
Cooking: 20 minutes

4 to 6 skinless, boneless chicken breast halves

½ cup all-purpose flour

1 tablespoon vegetable oil

1 tablespoon butter

1¾ cups Swanson® Chicken Broth (Regular, Natural Goodness™ **or** Certified Organic)

⅓ cup orange juice

¼ cup Chablis **or** other dry white wine

1 tablespoon grated orange peel

1 tablespoon chopped fresh sage leaves **or** 1 teaspoon ground sage

1 container (3.5 ounces) shiitake mushrooms, chopped (about 2 cups)

Hot cooked rice

1. Coat the chicken with the flour.

2. Heat the oil and butter in a 12-inch skillet over medium-high heat. Add the chicken and cook for 10 minutes or until it's well browned on both sides. Remove the chicken and set aside.

3. Stir the broth, juice, wine, peel and sage into the skillet. Heat to a boil.

4. Add the mushrooms. Return the chicken to the skillet and reduce the heat to low. Cook for 5 minutes or until the chicken is cooked through* and liquid has reduced by one-fourth. Serve with the rice.

*The internal temperature of the chicken should reach 160°F.

Lemon Olive Chicken

Makes 6 servings

- **1 tablespoon vegetable oil**
- **4 to 6 skinless, boneless chicken breast halves**
- **1 can (10¾ ounces) Campbell's® Condensed Cream of Chicken Soup (Regular or 98% Fat Free)**
- **¼ cup milk**
- **1 tablespoon lemon juice**
- **⅛ teaspoon ground black pepper**
- **½ cup sliced pimiento-stuffed Spanish olives**
- **4 lemon slices**
  Hot cooked rice

START TO FINISH:
25 minutes

Prepping: 10 minutes
Cooking: 15 minutes

1. Heat the oil in a 10-inch skillet over medium-high heat. Add the chicken and cook for 10 minutes or until it's well browned on both sides. Remove the chicken and set aside.

2. Stir the soup, milk, lemon juice, black pepper and olives into the skillet. Heat to a boil. Return the chicken to the skillet and reduce the heat to low. Top the chicken with the lemon slices. Cover and cook for 5 minutes or until the chicken is cooked through*. Serve with the rice.

The internal temperature of the chicken should reach 160°F.

Poultry

Wild Mushroom Chicken Balsamico

Makes 6 servings

START TO FINISH:
40 minutes

Prepping: 10 minutes
Cooking: 30 minutes

3 teaspoons olive **or** vegetable oil

4 to 6 skinless, boneless chicken breast halves

12 ounces assorted wild mushrooms (portobello, shiitake, oyster **and/or** cremini), sliced (about 3 cups)

1 medium zucchini, sliced (about 1½ cups)

1 medium onion, cut into wedges

2 cloves garlic, minced

2 cups Prego® Marinara Italian Sauce

¼ cup balsamic vinegar

Freshly ground black pepper

1. Heat **1 teaspoon** of the oil in a 12-inch nonstick skillet over medium-high heat. Add the chicken and cook for 10 minutes or until it's well browned on both sides. Remove the chicken and set aside.

2. Reduce the heat to medium and add the remaining oil. Add the mushrooms, zucchini and onion. Cook and stir until tender. Add garlic and cook for 1 minute.

3. Stir the Italian sauce and vinegar into the skillet. Heat to a boil. Return the chicken to the skillet and reduce the heat to low. Cover and cook for 10 minutes or until the chicken is cooked through*. Serve with the black pepper.

The internal temperature of the chicken should reach 160°F.

Rosemary Chicken & Mushroom Pasta

Makes 6 servings

2 tablespoons olive **or** vegetable oil

1½ pounds skinless, boneless chicken breasts, cut into strips

4 cups sliced mushrooms (about 12 ounces)

1 tablespoon minced garlic

1 tablespoon chopped fresh rosemary leaves **or** 1 teaspoon dried rosemary leaves, crushed

1 can (14½ ounces) Campbell's® Chicken Gravy

1 package (16 ounces) linguine **or** spaghetti, cooked and drained

Shredded Parmesan cheese

START TO FINISH:
30 minutes

Prepping: 10 minutes
Cooking: 20 minutes

1. Heat the oil in a 12-inch skillet over medium-high heat. Add the chicken and mushrooms and cook in 2 batches or until it's well browned, stirring often. Remove the chicken and mushrooms and set them aside.

2. Reduce the heat to low. Stir the garlic and rosemary into the skillet and cook for 1 minute. Stir the gravy into the skillet. Heat to a boil.

3. Return the chicken and mushrooms to the skillet. Cover and cook for 5 minutes or until the chicken is cooked through*. Place the pasta in a 3-quart serving bowl. Pour the chicken mixture over the pasta. Toss to coat. Serve with the cheese.

*The internal temperature of the chicken should reach 160°F.

Poultry

Turkey & Broccoli Alfredo

Makes 4 servings

START TO FINISH:
15 minutes

Prepping/Cooking:
15 minutes

Easy Substitution Tip:
Substitute spaghetti for the linguine and cooked chicken for the turkey.

½ of a 16 ounce package linguine

1 cup fresh **or** frozen broccoli flowerets

1 can (10¾ ounces) Campbell's® Condensed Cream of Mushroom Soup (Regular **or** 98% Fat Free)

½ cup milk

½ cup grated Parmesan cheese

¼ teaspoon ground black pepper

2 cups cubed cooked turkey

1. Prepare the linguine according to the package directions. Add the broccoli during the last 4 minutes of the cooking time. Drain the linguine and broccoli well in a colander and return them to the saucepot.

2. Stir the soup, milk, cheese, black pepper and turkey into the linguine and broccoli. Cook and stir over medium heat until hot and bubbling. Serve with additional cheese.

Tuscan Turkey & Beans

Makes 4 servings

- 2 tablespoons olive **or** vegetable oil
- 4 turkey breast cutlets **or** slices (about 1 pound)
- 1 medium onion, chopped (about ½ cup)
- 2 cloves garlic, minced
- 1½ teaspoons Italian seasoning, crushed
- 1 can (about 14½ ounces) diced tomatoes, undrained
- 1½ cups packed chopped fresh spinach leaves
- 1 can (10¾ ounces) Campbell's® Condensed Cream of Celery Soup (Regular **or** 98% Fat Free)
- ¼ teaspoon ground black pepper
- 1 can (about 15 ounces) white kidney (cannellini) beans, rinsed and drained
  Grated Parmesan cheese

**START TO FINISH:
30 minutes**

Prepping: 10 minutes
Cooking: 20 minutes

1. Heat **1 tablespoon** of the oil in a 12-inch skillet over medium heat. Add the turkey in 2 batches and cook 3 minutes or until the turkey is lightly browned on both sides. Remove the turkey and keep it warm.

2. Reduce the heat to medium and add the remaining oil. Add the onion, garlic and Italian seasoning and cook until the onion is tender-crisp, stirring often.

3. Add the tomatoes and spinach and cook just until the spinach wilts, stirring occasionally.

4. Stir the soup, black pepper and beans into the skillet. Heat to a boil. Return the turkey to the skillet and reduce the heat to low. Cover and cook for 5 minutes or until the turkey is cooked through*. Sprinkle with the cheese.

The internal temperature of the turkey should reach 160°F.

Herb Roasted Turkey

Makes 12 to 14 servings

START TO FINISH:
4 hours,
55 minutes

Prepping: 15 minutes
Roasting: 4 hours,
   30 minutes
Standing: 10 minutes

Leftover Tip:
Create inventive sandwiches with leftover turkey by spreading the bread with cranberry sauce or apple butter, then topping with turkey slices, fresh greens and chopped walnuts.

1¾ cups Swanson® Chicken Broth (Regular, Natural Goodness™ or Certified Organic)
   3 tablespoons lemon juice
   1 teaspoon dried basil leaves, crushed
   1 teaspoon dried thyme leaves, crushed
   ⅛ teaspoon ground black pepper
      12- to 14-pound turkey
   2 cans (14½ ounces **each**) Campbell's® Turkey Gravy

1. Stir the broth, lemon juice, basil, thyme and black pepper in a medium bowl.

2. Roast the turkey according to the package directions*, basting occasionally with the broth mixture. Let the turkey stand for 10 minutes before slicing. Discard any remaining broth mixture.

3. Heat the gravy in a 2-quart saucepan over medium heat until it's hot. Serve the turkey with the gravy.

The internal temperature of the turkey should reach 180°F.

Thawing Poultry

Safe defrosting of frozen chicken and turkey is an important part of preventing foodborne illness. Ideally, you should defrost the bird in the refrigerator. (This could take two or four days, depending on the size.) But if that's not possible, try using the cold-water method.

Wrap food in leak-proof plastic and place it in a bowl or sink full of cold water. Drain the water; then fill bowl or sink again with cold water. See the chart below for thawing times for both the refrigerator and the cold-water methods.

Thawing Times for Poultry

Type of Poultry	Thawing Time (refrigerator)	Thawing Time (cold-water)
Chicken, whole (3 to 4 pounds)	24 hours	1½ to 2 hours
Chicken, cut up (up to 4 pounds)	3 to 9 hours	1½ to 2 hours
Turkey, whole (up to 12 pounds)	1 to 2 days	4 to 6 hours
(12 to 16 pounds)	2 to 3 days	6 to 8 hours
(16 to 20 pounds)	3 to 4 days	8 to 10 hours
Turkey, cut up (up to 4 pounds)	3 to 9 hours	1½ to 2 hours

Thawing Tips:

• Poultry should not be thawed on the countertop at room temperature since the outside of the food will thaw quicker than the inside. This can result in food that is unsafe to eat. Poultry is best when thawed at a safe constant temperature in the refrigerator—40°F.

• Thaw chicken and turkey completely so you can be ensured it will cook thoroughly. To determine whether the bird is fully defrosted, look inside the cavity—ice crystals mean it needs more thaw time.

• Thawed poultry should be cooked within 24 hours. Refrigerate if you are not cooking it immediately after thawing. Do not refreeze.

• Take out giblets from the cavity as soon as they're defrosted enough to remove.

• If choosing to defrost in the microwave, follow the manufacturer's directions—microwave defrosting can be tricky since it is difficult to determine the proper defrosting times. If using the microwave to defrost, cook immediately after defrosting because some of the edges of the poultry may actually have begun cooking during defrosting.

Turkey Cutlets with Stuffing & Cranberry

Makes 8 servings

1 bag (14 ounces) Pepperidge Farm® Cubed Herb Seasoned Stuffing

1 stick (½ cup) butter

1 stalk celery, chopped (about ½ cup)

1 medium onion, chopped (about ½ cup)

1¾ cups Swanson® Chicken Broth (Regular, Natural Goodness™ **or** Certified Organic)

1 can (16 ounces) whole cranberry sauce

8 turkey breast cutlets **or** slices (about 2 pounds)

1 can (10¾ ounces) Campbell's® Condensed Cream of Chicken Soup (Regular **or** 98% Fat Free)

⅓ cup milk

START TO FINISH:
1 hour, 20 minutes

Prepping: 15 minutes
Baking: 1 hour,
5 minutes

Easy Substitution Tip:

Substitute a whole turkey London broil (about 2 pounds) and cut it into 8 cutlets for the packaged turkey cutlets.

1. Coarsely crush some of the stuffing to make **1 cup** stuffing. Set aside.

2. Heat the butter in 4-quart saucepan over medium heat. Add the celery and onion and cook until the tender.

3. Stir in the broth. Heat to a boil. Remove from the heat. Add the remaining stuffing and stir lightly to coat.

4. Spoon stuffing mixture into a 13×9-inch baking pan. Spread the cranberry sauce over the stuffing. Top with the turkey.

5. Stir the soup and milk in a small bowl. Pour over the turkey. Sprinkle with the reserved stuffing crumbs.

6. Bake at 375°F. for 1 hour, 5 minutes or until turkey is cooked through*.

The internal temperature of the turkey should reach 160°F.

Meat

Beef Stroganoff

Makes 4 servings

- **1 pound boneless beef sirloin or top round steak, ¾-inch thick**
- **Cracked black pepper**
- **1 tablespoon vegetable oil**
- **1 medium onion, finely chopped (about ½ cup)**
- **1 can (10¾ ounces) Campbell's® Condensed Cream of Mushroom Soup (Regular or 98% Fat Free)**
- **½ cup water**
- **¼ cup dry sherry (optional)**
- **1 tablespoon tomato paste**
- **¼ cup plain yogurt**
- **Hot cooked egg noodles**
- **Chopped fresh parsley**

1. Cut the beef into 2-inch pieces. Coat the beef with the black pepper.

2. Heat the oil in a 10-inch skillet over medium-high heat. Add the beef and cook until it's well browned on all sides, stirring often. Remove the beef with a slotted spoon and set it aside.

3. Reduce the heat to medium. Add the onion. Cook and stir until the onion is tender.

4. Stir the soup, water, sherry, if desired, and tomato paste into the skillet. Heat to a boil. Return the beef to the skillet and heat through. Remove from the heat. Stir in the yogurt. Serve over the noodles and sprinkle with the parsley.

Pan-Seared Beef Steaks with Garlic Red Wine Gravy

Makes 8 servings

START TO FINISH:
25 minutes

Prepping: 10 minutes
Cooking: 15 minutes

3 teaspoons butter

8 filet mignons (tenderloin steaks), ¾-inch thick (about 5 ounces each)

½ cup chopped shallots **or** onion

1 clove garlic, minced

1 can (10¼ ounces) Campbell's® Beef Gravy

½ cup dry red wine

1. Heat **1 teaspoon** of the butter in a 12-inch skillet over high heat. Add **4** steaks and cook for 4 minutes for medium-rare* or to desired doneness, turning the steaks over halfway through cooking. Remove the steaks. Cover and keep warm. Repeat with **1 teaspoon** butter and the remaining steaks.

2. Reduce the heat to medium and add the remaining butter. Add the shallots and cook for 1 minute. Add the garlic and cook for 30 seconds.

3. Stir the gravy and wine into the skillet. Heat to a boil. Return the steaks to the skillet and heat through.

The internal temperature of the steaks should reach 145°F.

Japanese Beef Stir Fry

Makes 8 servings

- 3 **tablespoons cornstarch**
- 1 **can (10½ ounces) Campbell's® Condensed Beef Broth**
- ½ **cup soy sauce**
- 2 **tablespoons sugar**
- 2 **tablespoons vegetable oil**
- 2 **pounds boneless beef sirloin or top round steak,**
  ¾-inch thick, cut in thin strips
- 4 **cups sliced shiitake mushrooms (about 7 ounces)**
- 1 **head Chinese cabbage (bok choy), thinly sliced**
  (about 6 cups)
- 2 **medium red peppers, cut into 2-inch-long strips**
  (about 3 cups)
- 3 **stalks celery, sliced (about 1½ cups)**
- 2 **medium green onions, cut into 2-inch**
  pieces (about ½ cup)
  Hot cooked rice

START TO FINISH:
50 minutes

Prepping: 30 minutes
Cooking: 20 minutes

Make Ahead Tip:
Prepare the vegetables
and place in resealable
plastic bags. Refrigerate
overnight.

1. Stir the cornstarch, broth, soy and sugar in a
small bowl. Set the mixture aside.

2. Heat **1 tablespoon** of the oil in a 4-quart
saucepan or wok over high heat. Add the beef in
2 batches and stir-fry until it's browned. Remove
the beef with a slotted spoon and set it aside.

3. Reduce the heat to medium and add the
remaining oil. Add the mushrooms, cabbage,
peppers, celery and green onions in 2 batches.
Stir-fry until the vegetables are tender-crisp.
Remove the vegetables with a slotted spoon and set
them aside.

4. Stir the cornstarch mixture and stir it into the saucepan. Cook and
stir until the mixture boils and thickens. Return the beef and
vegetables to the saucepan and cook until the mixture is hot and
bubbling. Serve over rice.

Meat

Rosemary Lamb Chops with Lemon Sauce

Makes 3 servings

**START TO FINISH:
18 to 21 minutes**

Prepping: 5 minutes
Broiling: 8 to
 11 minutes
Cooking: 5 minutes

6 lamb chops (about ¾-inch thick)

1 teaspoon dried rosemary leaves, crushed

1 teaspoon cornstarch

1 cup Swanson® Chicken Broth (Regular, Natural Goodness™ **or** Certified Organic)

3 tablespoons lemon juice

1 tablespoon Dijon-style mustard

¾ teaspoon finely chopped lemon peel

1. Heat the broiler*. Season the lamb chops with the rosemary. Put the chops on a rack in a broiler pan.

2. Broil the chops with the top of the chops 3 to 4 inches from the heat for 8 to 11 minutes** (for medium-rare) or until the lamb is cooked to desired doneness, turning the chops with kitchen tongs halfway through cooking.

3. Stir the cornstarch, broth, lemon juice, mustard and lemon peel in a 1-quart saucepan. Cook and stir over medium heat until the mixture boils and thickens. Spoon the lemon sauce over the chops.

*To grill the lamb chops, lightly oil the grill rack and heat the grill to medium. Grill the chops for 8 to 11 minutes** or until desired doneness.
**The internal temperature of the lamb should reach 145°F.

Beef & Bean Burritos

Makes 8 burritos

1 pound ground beef

1 small onion, chopped (about ¼ cup)

1 can (11¼ ounces) Campbell's® Condensed Fiesta Chili Beef Soup

¼ cup water

8 flour tortillas (8-inch), warmed

Shredded Cheddar cheese

Pace® Chunky Salsa

Sour cream

**START TO FINISH:
20 minutes**

Prepping: 5 minutes
Cooking: 15 minutes

1. Cook the beef and onion in a 10-inch skillet over medium-high heat until the beef is well browned, stirring frequently to break up the meat. Pour off any fat.

2. Stir the soup and water into the skillet. Reduce the heat to low. Cook and stir until the mixture is hot and bubbling.

3. Spoon about ⅓ **cup** of the beef mixture down the center of each tortilla. Top with cheese, salsa and sour cream. Fold the sides of the tortilla over the filling and then fold up the ends to enclose the filling.

Herbed Beef & Vegetable Skillet

Makes 4 servings

START TO FINISH:
30 minutes

Prepping: 10 minutes
Cooking: 20 minutes

2 tablespoons vegetable **or** canola oil

1 pound boneless beef sirloin **or** top round steak, ¾-inch thick, cut into thin strips

3 medium carrots, sliced thin diagonally (about 1½ cups)

1 medium onion, chopped (about ½ cup)

2 cloves garlic, minced

½ teaspoon dried thyme leaves, crushed

1 can (10¾ ounces) Campbell's® Condensed Golden Mushroom Soup

¼ cup water

2 teaspoons Worcestershire sauce

⅛ teaspoon ground black pepper

Hot cooked noodles

1. Heat **1 tablespoon** of the oil in a 12-inch skillet over medium-high heat. Add the beef and cook and stir until it's well browned. Remove the beef with a slotted spoon and set it aside.

2. Reduce the heat to medium and add the remaining oil. Add the carrots, onion, garlic and thyme. Cook and stir until the vegetables are tender-crisp.

3. Stir the soup, water, Worcestershire and black pepper into the skillet. Heat to a boil. Return the beef to the skillet and cook until the mixture is hot and bubbling. Serve over the noodles.

Sliced Steak Pizzaiola

Makes 6 servings

1 tablespoon vegetable oil
1½ pounds beef flank steak
2 medium onions, sliced (about 1 cup)
2 cloves garlic, minced
1 teaspoon Italian seasoning, crushed
2 cups Prego® Traditional Italian Sauce

START TO FINISH:
20 minutes

Prepping/Cooking:
20 minutes

1. Heat the oil in a 10-inch skillet over medium-high heat. Add the steak and cook for 8 minutes or until it's browned on both sides. Remove the steak from the skillet and set it aside.

2. Reduce the heat to medium. Add the onions, garlic and Italian seasoning. Cook and stir until the vegetables are tender.

3. Stir the Italian sauce into the skillet. Heat to a boil. Return the steak to the skillet. Reduce the heat to low. Cover and cook until desired doneness (3 minutes for medium-rare*).

4. Cut the steak into thin diagonal slices. Serve with the sauce.

The internal temperature of the steak should reach 145°F.

Meat

Simple Salisbury Steak

Makes 4 servings

START TO FINISH:
30 minutes

Prepping: 5 minutes
Cooking: 25 minutes

Time-Saving Tip:
To speed up meal preparation, do some of the work ahead. Shape the burgers, cover and refrigerate. You can also save time by purchasing chopped onions and sliced mushrooms.

1 **pound ground beef**
1 **can (10¾ ounces) Campbell's® Condensed Cream of Mushroom Soup (Regular or 98% Fat Free)**
⅓ **cup dry bread crumbs**
1 **egg, beaten**
1 **small onion, finely chopped (about ¼ cup)**
1 **tablespoon vegetable oil**
1½ **cups sliced mushrooms**

1. Thoroughly mix the beef, ¼ cup of the soup, bread crumbs, egg and onion in a medium bowl. Shape the mixture into 4 (½-inch thick) burgers.

2. Heat the oil in a 10-inch skillet over medium-high heat. Add the burgers and cook until well browned on both sides. Remove the burgers with a slotted spatula and set aside.

3. Stir the remaining soup and mushrooms into the skillet. Heat to a boil. Return the burgers to the skillet and reduce the heat to low. Cover and cook for 10 minutes or until the burgers are cooked through*.

The internal temperature of the burgers should reach 160°F.

Holiday Brisket with Savory Onion Jus

Makes 8 servings

2 tablespoons olive **or** vegetable oil

6 medium onions, cut into quarters (about 6 cups)

1 butternut squash (about 2½ pounds), peeled, seeded and cut into 1½-inch cubes (about 6 cups)

3-pound boneless beef brisket

1¾ cups Swanson® Beef Broth (Regular, Lower Sodium **or** Certified Organic)

½ cup orange juice

½ cup dry red wine

½ cup packed brown sugar

1 can (28 ounces) whole peeled tomatoes

START TO FINISH:
3 hours, 40 minutes

Prepping: 15 minutes
Cooking: 3 hours, 15 minutes
Standing: 10 minutes

1. Heat the oil in a 4-quart saucepan over medium-high heat. Add the onions and squash and cook until tender-crisp. Remove the vegetables with a slotted spoon and set them aside.

2. Season brisket as desired. Add the brisket to the saucepan and cook until it's well browned on all sides.

3. Add the broth, orange juice, wine, brown sugar and tomatoes into the saucepan. Heat to a boil. Spoon broth mixture over the brisket. Reduce the heat to low. Cover and cook for 2 hours.

4. Return the vegetables to the pan. Cover and cook for 1 hour more or until the meat is fork-tender, stirring occasionally.

5. Remove the brisket from the pan to a cutting board and let it stand for 10 minutes. Thinly slice brisket across the grain and arrange on a serving platter. Remove the vegetables with a slotted spoon and put on platter. Pour the pan juices into a gravy boat and serve with the brisket.

Savory Pot Roast & Harvest Vegetables

Makes 6 servings

START TO FINISH:
2 hours, 45 minutes

Prepping: 15 minutes
Cooking: 2 hours,
30 minutes

Easy Substitution Tip:
Substitute Calcium
Enriched V8® or
100% Vitamins A, C
& E V8® for the
100% Vegetable Juice.

2 tablespoons vegetable oil
3-pound boneless beef bottom round **or** chuck pot roast
1¾ cups Swanson® Seasoned Beef Broth with Onion
¾ cup V8® 100% Vegetable Juice
3 medium potatoes (about ¾ pound), cut into quarters
3 stalks celery, cut into 1-inch pieces (about 2¼ cups)
2 cups fresh **or** frozen baby carrots
2 tablespoons all-purpose flour
¼ cup water

1. Heat the oil in a 4-quart saucepan over medium-high heat. Add the roast and cook until it's well browned on all sides. Pour off any fat.

2. Add the broth and vegetable juice. Heat to a boil. Reduce the heat to low. Cover and cook for 1 hour, 45 minutes.

3. Add the potatoes, celery and carrots. Cover and cook for 30 minutes more or until the meat and vegetables are fork-tender. Remove the roast and vegetables to a serving platter.

4. Stir the flour and water in a small cup and stir into the broth mixture. Cook and stir over medium-high heat until the mixture boils and thickens. Serve with roast and vegetables.

Irish Spiced Beef

Makes 8 servings

3 tablespoons packed brown sugar

2 teaspoons ground cloves

2 teaspoons ground allspice

2 teaspoons ground cinnamon

1 teaspoon cracked black pepper

4-pound boneless beef bottom round **or** chuck pot roast

1¾ cups Swanson® Beef Broth (Regular, Lower Sodium **or** Certified Organic)

1 bottle (12 fluid ounces) stout **or** dark beer

Hot boiled potatoes (optional)

Chopped fresh parsley

START TO FINISH: 15 hours, 15 minutes

Prepping: 5 minutes
Marinating: 12 hours
Baking: 3 hours
Standing: 10 minutes

1. Mix the brown sugar, cloves, allspice, cinnamon and pepper in a large bowl. Add the roast and turn it to coat with the spice mixture. Cover and refrigerate for at least 12 hours or overnight.

2. Remove the roast and place it in an oven-safe 4-quart saucepan.

3. Add the broth and beer. Cover and bake at 350°F. for 3 hours or until the meat is fork-tender.

4. Remove the roast from the pan to a cutting board and let it stand for 10 minutes. Thinly slice the roast and arrange on a serving platter. Pour the pan juices into a gravy boat and serve with the roast beef. Serve with boiled potatoes, if desired. Sprinkle with parsley.

Campbell's Kitchen Tip:
For even more flavorful potatoes, cook peeled, medium potatoes in Swanson® Chicken Broth (Regular, Natural Goodness™ or Certified Organic).

Time-Saving Tip:
For easy cleanup, use a resealable heavy-duty plastic bag instead of a bowl.

Steak & Mushroom Florentine

Makes 4 servings

START TO FINISH:
20 minutes

Prepping/Cooking:
20 minutes

2 tablespoons vegetable oil

1 pound boneless beef sirloin **or** top round steak, ¾-inch thick, cut into thin strips

1 small onion, sliced (about ¼ cup)

4 cups baby spinach leaves, washed

1 can (10¾ ounces) Campbell's® Condensed Cream of Mushroom Soup (Regular **or** 98% Fat Free)

1 cup water

1 large tomato, thickly sliced

Freshly ground black pepper

1. Heat **1 tablespoon** of the oil in a 10-inch nonstick skillet over medium-high heat. Add the beef and cook and stir until it's well browned. Remove the beef with a slotted spoon and set it aside.

2. Reduce the heat to medium and add the remaining oil. Add the onion. Cook and stir until onion is tender-crisp. Add the spinach and cook just until the spinach wilts.

3. Stir the soup and water into the skillet. Heat to a boil. Return the beef to the skillet and cook until the mixture is hot and bubbling. Serve over the tomato. Season to taste with black pepper.

Sloppy Joe Pizza

Makes 4 servings

¾ **pound ground beef**

1 **can (10¾ ounces) Campbell's® Condensed Tomato Soup**

1 **Italian bread shell (12-inch)**

1½ **cups shredded Cheddar cheese (6 ounces)**

**START TO FINISH:
22 minutes**

Prepping/Cooking:
10 minutes
Baking: 12 minutes

1. Heat the oven to 450°F.

2. Cook the beef in a 10-inch skillet over medium-high heat until the beef is well browned, stirring frequently to break up meat. Pour off any fat.

3. Stir the soup into the skillet. Reduce the heat to low and cook until the mixture is hot and bubbling.

4. Spread the beef mixture over the shell to within ¼-inch of the edge. Top with the cheese.

5. Bake for 12 minutes or until the cheese melts.

Saucy Creole Pork Chops

Makes 4 servings

START TO FINISH:
30 minutes

Prepping: 5 minutes
Cooking: 25 minutes

4 boneless pork chops, ¾-inch thick (about 1 pound)
1½ teaspoons Creole **or** Cajun seasoning
2 tablespoons vegetable **or** canola oil
1 medium onion, chopped (about ½ cup)
2 cloves garlic, minced
1 can (10¾ ounces) Campbell's Condensed Cream of Celery Soup (Regular **or** 98% Fat Free)
⅓ cup water
1 tablespoon chopped fresh parsley
1 can (14½ ounces) diced tomatoes, undrained
Hot cooked rice

1. Season the pork chops with the Creole seasoning.

2. Heat **1 tablespoon** of the oil in a 10-inch skillet over medium-high heat. Add the pork chops and cook until they're well browned on both sides. Remove the chops and set them aside.

3. Reduce the heat to medium and add the remaining oil. Add the onion and garlic. Cook and stir until the onion is tender-crisp. Pour off any fat.

4. Stir the soup, water, parsley and tomatoes into the skillet. Heat to a boil. Return the pork chops to the skillet and cook for 5 minutes or until the chops are slightly pink in the center*. Serve with the rice.

*The internal temperature of the pork should reach 160°F.

Cassoulet

Makes 8 servings

- 4 slices thick-cut bacon (about 4 ounces), diced
- 1 pound **each** boneless leg of lamb **and** boneless pork loin, cut into 1-inch pieces
- ½ pound kielbasa, sliced diagonally
- ¼ cup chopped fresh parsley
- 3 cloves garlic, minced
- 2 tablespoons grated lemon peel (about 1 lemon)
- 1 teaspoon dried thyme leaves, crushed
- 2 cans (15 ounces **each**) great Northern beans, rinsed and drained
- 2 bay leaves
- 1 can (14½ ounces) Campbell's® Beef Gravy
- 1 cup Swanson® Beef Broth (Regular, Lower Sodium **or** Certified Organic)
- 2 tablespoons tomato paste
- ½ cup dry bread crumbs

START TO FINISH:
10 hours,
20 minutes

Prepping: 20 minutes
Baking: 2 hours
Refrigerating: 8 hours

Time-Saving Tip:
To save prep time, ask your butcher to cut the lamb and pork into 1-inch pieces.

Make Ahead Tip:
Cassoulet is best when prepared and fully cooked the day ahead. Refrigerate. To reheat, bake at 300°F. for 1 hour or until hot. Add additional Swanson® Beef Broth to keep beans from drying out.

1. Cook bacon in a 6-quart oven-safe saucepot over medium-high heat for 5 minutes or until the bacon is crisp. Remove the bacon with a slotted spoon and drain on paper towels.

2. Add the lamb, pork and kielbasa in 2 batches and cook in the hot drippings until well browned. Remove with a slotted spoon and set the lamb, pork and kielbasa aside.

3. Stir the parsley, garlic, lemon peel and thyme in a small cup.

4. Layer **1 cup** of the beans, **half** of **each** of the bacon, lamb, pork, sausage, parsley mixture and **1** bay leaf in the saucepot. Repeat layers, using **half** the remaining beans. Top with remaining beans.

5. Stir the gravy, broth and tomato paste in a small bowl. Pour the gravy mixture over meat and beans.

6. Bake at 350°F. for 1 hour. Sprinkle with bread crumbs. Bake for 1 hour more or until lamb is fork-tender. Discard the bay leaves. Serve immediately or cool 2 hours, cover and refrigerate at least 8 hours or overnight.

Meat

Sausage-Stuffed Green Peppers

Makes 8 servings

START TO FINISH:
1 hour

Prepping: 20 minutes
Baking: 40 minutes

4 medium green peppers

1 tablespoon vegetable oil

1 pound sweet Italian pork sausage, casing removed

1 teaspoon dried oregano leaves, crushed

1 medium onion, chopped (about ½ cup)

1 cup shredded part-skim mozzarella cheese (4 ounces)

2 cups Prego® Traditional Italian Sauce

1. Cut a thin slice from the top of each pepper, cut in half lengthwise and discard the seeds and white membranes. Place the pepper shells in a 13×9×2-inch shallow baking dish or roasting pan and set them aside.

2. Heat the oil in a 10-inch skillet over medium-high heat. Add the sausage and cook until it's well browned, stirring to break up the meat. Add the oregano and onion and cook until the onion is tender. Pour off any fat. Stir in the cheese.

3. Spoon the sausage mixture into the pepper shells. Pour the Italian sauce over the peppers. Cover the dish with foil.

4. Bake at 400°F. for 40 minutes or until the sausage reaches an internal temperature of 160°F. and the peppers are tender.

Roast Pork with Green Apples & Golden Squash

Makes 8 servings

Vegetable cooking spray

2 (¾ pound **each**) whole pork tenderloins

1 teaspoon olive oil

¼ teaspoon coarsely ground black pepper

3 large Granny Smith apples, cored and thickly sliced

1 butternut squash (about 1½ pounds), peeled, seeded and cubed (about 4 cups)

2 tablespoons packed brown sugar

½ teaspoon ground cinnamon

1¾ cups Swanson® Chicken Broth (Regular, Natural Goodness™ **or** Certified Organic)

2 teaspoons all-purpose flour

START TO FINISH:
1 hour, 15 minutes

Prepping: 20 minutes
Baking: 45 minutes
Standing: 10 minutes

1. Heat the oven to 425°F. Spray a 17×11-inch roasting pan with cooking spray.

2. Brush the pork with the oil and sprinkle with the black pepper. Put the pork in the prepared pan.

3. Put the apples, squash, brown sugar, cinnamon and ½ **cup** broth in a large bowl. Toss to coat with the broth mixture. Add the squash mixture to the pan.

4. Bake for 25 minutes or until cooked through but slightly pink in center*, stirring the squash mixture once while it's cooking. Remove the pork from the pan to a cutting board and let it stand for 10 minutes. Continue to bake the squash mixture for 15 minutes more or until browned. Remove the squash mixture from the pan with a slotted spoon.

5. Stir the flour into the drippings in the roasting pan. Cook and stir over medium heat for 1 minute then gradually stir in the remaining broth. Cook and stir until the mixture boils and thickens. Thinly slice the pork and arrange on a serving platter with the vegetables. Pour the sauce into a gravy boat and serve with the pork.

The internal temperature of the pork should reach 155°F. During the standing time, the temperature will continue to increase to 160°F.

Meat

Polynesian Pork Chops

Makes 4 servings

START TO FINISH:
20 minutes

Prepping/Cooking:
20 minutes

4 boneless pork chops, ¾-inch thick (about 1 pound)
1 teaspoon garlic powder
1 tablespoon vegetable oil
1 can (10¾ ounces) Campbell's® Condensed Golden Mushroom Soup
¼ cup water
1 can (8 ounces) pineapple chunks, undrained
1 medium onion, chopped (about ½ cup)
3 tablespoons soy sauce
1 tablespoon honey
Hot cooked rice
Sliced green onions

1. Season the pork chops with the garlic powder.

2. Heat the oil in a 10-inch skillet over medium-high heat. Add the pork chops and cook until they're well browned on both sides.

3. Add the soup, water, pineapple with juice, onion, soy and honey. Heat to a boil. Reduce the heat to low. Cover and cook for 10 minutes or until the chops are slightly pink in the center*. Serve with the rice and sprinkle with the green onions.

The internal temperature of the pork should reach 160°F.

Cherry & Port Glazed Ham

Makes 14 to 20 servings

1 tablespoon cornstarch

3½ cups Swanson® Chicken Broth (Regular, Natural Goodness™ **or** Certified Organic)

2 tablespoons butter

⅓ cup chopped shallots

⅛ teaspoon ground allspice

1 cup port **or** other sweet red wine

1 bag (5 ounces) dried cherries (about 1 cup)

⅓ cup packed brown sugar

7- to 10-pound unglazed fully-cooked bone-in spiral-sliced ham

1 turkey-size oven cooking bag (19×23½ inches)

1. Stir the cornstarch and broth in a medium bowl. Set the mixture aside.

2. Heat the butter in a 12-inch skillet over medium heat. Add the shallots and cook until tender. Add the allspice and cook for 30 seconds.

3. Stir the wine, cherries and brown sugar into the skillet. Heat to a boil. Reduce the heat to low. Cook until slightly thickened, stirring occasionally.

4. Stir the cornstarch mixture and stir it into the skillet. Cook and stir until the mixture boils and thickens.

5. Unwrap the ham. Remove and discard the plastic disc covering the bone. Place the oven bag in a 13×9×2-inch baking pan. Place the ham in the bag. Pour the cherry glaze over the ham. Close the bag with the nylon tie. Cut 6 (½-inch) slits in the top of the bag.

6. Bake at 250°F. for 1½ to 2½ hours or until heated through*. Remove the ham from the bag and place on a serving platter. Spoon some of the cherry glaze over the ham and pour the remaining glaze into a gravy boat. Serve with the ham.

The internal temperature of the ham should reach 150°F.

START TO FINISH:
2 hours, 50 minutes

Prepping: 20 minutes
Baking: 2 hours, 30 minutes

Make Ahead Tip:
The Cherry Port Glaze can be cooled and refrigerated for up to 2 days. Reheat the glaze in a 2-quart saucepan over medium-low heat before pouring over the ham.

Thawing Beef and Pork

Defrosting meat safely is important but not difficult. Ideally, you should defrost the frozen meat in the refrigerator. (This could take several days, depending on the size.) But if that's not possible, try using the cold-water method.

Wrap food in leak-proof plastic and place it in a bowl or sink of cold water. Change the water every 20 to 30 minutes to keep it cold. See the chart below for thawing times for both the refrigerator and the cold-water methods.

Thawing Times for Beef

Type of Meat	Thawing Time (refrigerator)	Thawing Time (cold-water)
Ground beef (1 pound)	24 hours	1½ to 2½ hours
Ground beef patties (½-inch thick)	12 hours	1 hour or less
Steak (1-inch thick)	12 hours	1 hour or less
Steak (more than 1-inch thick)	up to 24 hours	1½ to 2½ hours
Pot Roast (thinner, such as chuck)	3 to 5 hours per pound	2 to 3 hours
Pot Roast (thicker, such as round)	4 to 7 hours per pound	30 minutes per pound

Thawing Times for Pork

Type of Meat	Thawing Time (refrigerator)	Thawing Time (cold-water)
Chops or Steaks (4-pack)	20 to 24 hours	1½ to 2½ hours
Single Chop or Steak	12 to 24 hours	1 hour or less
Roast (thinner, such as loin)	4 to 5 hours per pound	2 to 3 hours
Roast (thicker, such as shoulder)	5 to 7 hours per pound	30 minutes per pound

Thawing Tips:

• Don't thaw meats on the countertop at room temperature since the outside of the food will thaw more quickly than the inside. This can result in food that is unsafe to eat. It is safest when meats are thawed at a safe, constant temperature—at 40°F in the refrigerator.

• Thaw meats completely so they will cook thoroughly.

• Cook thawed meats within 24 hours of defrosting. Refrigerate if you are not cooking immediately after thawing. Do not refreeze.

• If you decide to defrost in the microwave, follow the manufacturer's directions. Microwave defrosting can be tricky since it is difficult to determine the proper defrosting times. Because defrosting in the microwave often begins to cook the edges of the meat, cook the thawed meat immediately.

Cranberry Dijon Pork Chops

Makes 4 servings

- **1 tablespoon olive oil**
- **4 boneless pork chops, 1-inch thick (about 1¼ pounds)**
- **1 can (10¾ ounces) Campbell's® Condensed Cream of Celery Soup (Regular or 98% Fat Free)**
- **½ cup cranberry juice**
- **2 tablespoons Dijon-style mustard**
- **¼ teaspoon dried thyme leaves, crushed**
- **¼ cup dried cranberries or cherries**
- **Hot cooked noodles**

**START TO FINISH:
55 minutes**

Prepping: 10 minutes
Cooking/Baking:
    45 minutes

1. Heat the oil in a 10-inch oven-safe skillet over medium-high heat. Add the pork chops and cook until the chops are well browned on both sides. Remove the pork chops and set them aside.

2. Stir the soup, cranberry juice, mustard and thyme into the skillet. Heat to a boil. Return the pork chops to the skillet and cover.

3. Bake at 350°F. for 45 minutes or until chops are cooked through but slightly pink in center*. Place the pork chops on a serving plate. Stir the cranberries into the skillet. Serve the sauce with the pork and noodles.

The internal temperature of the pork should reach 160°F.

Fish and Shellfish

START TO FINISH:
20 minutes

Prepping: 10 minutes
Baking: 10 minutes

Easy Substitution Tip:
Substitute about
2 pounds firm white fish
fillets such as cod,
haddock or halibut for
the tilapia fillets.

Italian Fish Fillets

Makes 8 servings

- 2 slices Pepperidge Farm® Sandwich White Bread, torn into pieces
- ⅓ cup shredded Parmesan cheese
- 1 clove garlic
- ½ teaspoon dried thyme leaves, crushed
- ⅛ teaspoon ground black pepper
- 2 tablespoons olive oil
- 8 fresh tilapia fish fillets (3 to 4 ounces **each**)
- 1 egg, beaten

1. Place the bread, cheese, garlic, thyme and black pepper in an electric blender container. Cover and blend until fine crumbs form. Slowly add the olive oil and blend until moistened.

2. Put the fish fillets in a 17×11-inch roasting pan. Brush with the egg. Divide the bread crumb mixture evenly over the fillets.

3. Bake at 400°F. for 10 minutes or until the fish flakes easily when tested with a fork and the crumb topping is golden.

Crab & Asparagus Risotto

Makes 8 servings

START TO FINISH:
40 minutes

Prepping/Cooking:
 10 minutes
Cooking: 25 minutes
Standing: 5 minutes

2 tablespoons olive oil

1 medium orange pepper, diced (about 1 cup)

½ cup chopped onion **or** shallots

2 cups **uncooked** Arborio rice (short-grain)

½ cup dry white wine

6 cups Swanson® Chicken Broth (Regular, Natural Goodness™ **or** Certified Organic), heated

½ pound asparagus **or** green beans, trimmed, cut into 1-inch pieces (about 1½ cups)

½ pound refrigerated pasteurized crabmeat (about 1½ cups)

Grated Parmesan cheese

1. Heat the oil in a 4-quart saucepan over medium heat. Add the pepper and onion and cook for 3 minutes or until the vegetables are tender. Add the rice and cook and stir for 2 minutes or until the rice is opaque.

2. Add the wine and cook and stir until it's absorbed. Stir **2 cups** of the hot broth into the rice mixture. Cook and stir until the broth is absorbed, maintaining the rice at a gentle simmer. Continue cooking and adding broth, ½ **cup** at a time, stirring until it's absorbed after each addition before adding more. Add the asparagus and crabmeat with the last broth addition.

3. Stir ¼ cup of the cheese into the risotto. Remove the saucepan from the heat. Cover and let it stand for 5 minutes. Serve the risotto with additional cheese.

Corn-Crusted Catfish

Makes 6 servings

1½ **cups buttermilk**

1 **teaspoon hot pepper sauce**

6 **fresh catfish fillets (6 ounces each)**

1½ **to 2 cups crushed Pepperidge Farm® Cornbread Stuffing**

Vegetable oil

Lemon wedges

Tartar sauce

1. Stir the buttermilk and hot sauce in a shallow bowl. Add the catfish fillets and turn to coat with the buttermilk mixture. Let marinate for 15 minutes. Remove the fish from the marinade. Place the stuffing on a plate. Coat both sides of the fish with the stuffing.

2. Pour the oil into a deep, heavy skillet to a depth of ¼-inch. Heat to about 370°F. Add the fish in 2 batches and cook for 6 to 8 minutes, carefully turning once or until the fish flakes easily when tested with a fork. Remove with a pancake turner and drain on paper towels. Serve the fish with the lemon and tartar sauce.

**START TO FINISH:
40 minutes**

Prepping: 5 minutes
Marinating:
15 minutes
Cooking: 20 minutes

Campbell's Kitchen Tip:
Place stuffing in resealable plastic bag and seal. Use a rolling pin and roll back and forth over bag until it's crushed.

Balsamic Glazed Salmon

Makes 8 servings

START TO FINISH:
25 minutes

Prepping: 5 minutes
Baking/Cooking:
  20 minutes

8 fresh salmon fillets, ¾-inch thick (about 1½ pounds)
  Freshly ground black pepper
3 tablespoons olive oil
4½ teaspoons cornstarch
1¾ cups Swanson® Chicken Broth (Regular, Natural Goodness™ or Certified Organic)
3 tablespoons balsamic vinegar
1 tablespoon orange juice
1 tablespoon brown sugar
1 teaspoon grated orange peel
  Orange slices for garnish

1. Place the salmon in a 12×8×2-inch shallow baking dish. Sprinkle with the black pepper and drizzle with the oil. Bake at 350°F. for 15 minutes or until the fish flakes easily when tested with a fork.

2. Stir the cornstarch, broth, vinegar, orange juice, brown sugar and orange peel in a 2-quart saucepan over high heat. Heat to a boil. Continue to cook until the mixture thickens, stirring constantly.

3. Place the salmon on a serving platter and serve with the sauce. Garnish with the orange slices.

Linguine with Easy Red Clam Sauce

Makes 4 servings

- **1** tablespoon olive **or** vegetable oil
- **2** cloves garlic, minced
- **1½** cups Prego® Traditional Italian Sauce
- **¼** cup Chablis **or** other dry white wine
- **1** tablespoon chopped fresh parsley
- **2** cans (6½ ounces **each**) minced clams, undrained
- **½** of a 16 ounce package linguine, cooked and drained
  Grated Parmesan cheese (optional)

**START TO FINISH:
25 minutes**

Prepping: 10 minutes
Cooking: 15 minutes

1. Heat the oil in a 2-quart saucepan over medium heat. Add the garlic and cook until tender, stirring constantly.

2. Stir the Italian sauce, wine, parsley and clams into the saucepan. Reduce the heat to low. Cover and cook for 10 minutes, stirring occasionally.

3. Serve the clam sauce over the linguine topped with the Parmesan cheese if desired.

Margarita Shrimp Salad

Makes 4 servings

START TO FINISH:
55 minutes

Marinating:
30 minutes
Prepping: 15 minutes
Cooking: 10 minutes

1 tablespoon lime juice

2 teaspoons grated lime peel

3 cloves garlic, minced

1 pound fresh large shrimp, shelled and deveined

¾ cup Swanson® Chicken Broth (Regular, Natural Goodness™ **or** Certified Organic)

1 medium orange **or** red pepper, cut into 2-inch-long strips (about 1½ cups)

1 small onion, sliced (about ¼ cup)

¼ cup chopped fresh cilantro leaves

4 cups torn romaine **or** iceberg lettuce

2 large tomatoes, thickly sliced

1. Stir the lime juice, lime peel and garlic in a 12×8×2-inch nonmetallic shallow baking dish or gallon size resealable plastic bag. Add the shrimp and toss to coat with the marinade. Cover the dish or seal the plastic bag and refrigerate it for 30 minutes, turning the shrimp over a few times while it's marinating.

2. Heat the broth in a 2-quart saucepan over high heat to a boil. Add the pepper and onion and cook until the vegetables are tender-crisp.

3. Reduce the heat to medium. Add the shrimp and marinade. Cook until the shrimp turn pink. Stir in the cilantro.

4. Divide the lettuce, tomatoes and shrimp mixture among 4 serving plates.

New Orleans Shrimp Toss

Makes 4 servings

- 2 tablespoons vegetable oil
- 2 tablespoons lemon juice
- 1 tablespoon Worcestershire sauce
- 1 teaspoon Cajun seasoning
- 1 pound fresh large shrimp, shelled and deveined
- 1 medium onion, chopped (about ½ cup)
- 2 cloves garlic, minced
- 1 can (10¾ ounces) Campbell's® Condensed Cream of Chicken with Herbs Soup
- ½ cup milk
- 1 teaspoon paprika
  Cornbread **or** biscuits
- 2 tablespoons chopped fresh chives

**START TO FINISH:
25 minutes**

Prepping: 10 minutes
Cooking: 15 minutes

1. Stir **1 tablespoon** of the oil, lemon juice, Worcestershire and Cajun seasoning in a medium bowl. Add the shrimp and toss lightly to coat.

2. Heat the remaining oil in a 10-inch skillet over medium-high heat. Add the onion and garlic. Cook and stir until the onion is tender.

3. Stir the soup, milk and paprika into the skillet. Heat to a boil. Add the shrimp mixture to the skillet and reduce the heat to low. Cover and cook for 5 minutes or until the shrimp turn pink. Serve with the cornbread and sprinkle with the chives.

Almond-Crusted Salmon with Thyme & Lemon Butter Sauce

Makes 8 servings

START TO FINISH:
40 minutes

Prepping: 15 minutes
Baking/Cooking:
  25 minutes

¼ cup unseasoned dry bread crumbs

¼ cup blanched almonds

1 clove garlic

2 tablespoons olive oil

8 fresh salmon fillets (about 3 pounds)

1 tablespoon cornstarch

1½ cups Swanson® Chicken Broth (Regular, Natural Goodness™ **or** Certified Organic)

2 tablespoons fresh lemon juice

1 teaspoon chopped fresh thyme leaves **or** ¼ teaspoon dried thyme leaves, crushed

3 tablespoons butter

¼ cup chopped shallots **or** onion

1. Put the bread crumbs, almonds and garlic in an electric blender or food processor container. Cover and blend until finely ground. With the blender running, slowly add the olive oil and blend until the crumbs are moist.

2. Arrange the salmon in a 17×11-inch roasting pan. Divide the bread crumb mixture evenly among the salmon fillets and gently press on the mixture so it adheres to the fish.

3. Bake at 400°F. for 15 minutes or until the fish flakes easily when tested with a fork and the topping is golden. Keep warm.

4. Stir the cornstarch, broth, lemon juice and thyme in a small bowl. Set the mixture aside.

5. Heat **2 tablespoons** of the butter in a 1-quart saucepan over medium heat. Add the shallots and cook until tender. Stir the cornstarch mixture and stir it into the skillet. Heat to a boil. Cook and stir until the mixture boils and thickens. Stir in the remaining butter until it melts. Serve the salmon with the sauce.

Poached Halibut with Pineapple Salsa

Makes 4 servings

START TO FINISH:
25 minutes

Prepping: 10 minutes
Cooking: 15 minutes

1 can (15¼ ounces) pineapple chunks in juice, undrained
1 seedless cucumber, peeled and diced (about 1⅔ cups)
1 medium red pepper, chopped (about ¾ cup)
2 tablespoons chopped red onion
1 teaspoon white wine vinegar
1 teaspoon hot pepper sauce (optional)
1¾ cups Swanson® Chicken Broth (Regular, Natural Goodness™ **or** Certified Organic)
¼ cup white wine
4 fresh halibut fillets (about 1½ pounds)

1. Drain the pineapple and reserve ⅔ cup juice.

2. Stir the pineapple chunks, cucumber, red pepper, red onion, vinegar and hot pepper sauce, if desired, in a medium bowl and set aside.

3. Heat the broth, wine and reserved pineapple juice in a 12-inch skillet over high heat to a boil. Add the fish and reduce the heat to low. Cover and cook for 10 minutes or until the fish flakes easily when tested with a fork. Serve the fish with the pineapple salsa.

Mediterranean Halibut with Couscous

Makes 4 servings

4 fresh halibut steaks, about 1-inch thick (about 1½ pounds)

¼ cup all-purpose flour

3 tablespoons olive oil

2 shallots, chopped

1 cup Swanson® Chicken Broth (Regular, Natural Goodness™ or Certified Organic)

2 teaspoons dried oregano leaves, crushed

1 can (14.5 ounces) diced tomatoes, drained

½ cup kalamata olives, pitted and sliced

1 package (10 ounces) **uncooked** couscous (about 1½ cups)

Additional Swanson® Chicken Broth (Regular, Natural Goodness™ **or** Certified Organic)

**START TO FINISH:
30 minutes**

Prepping: 15 minutes
Cooking: 15 minutes

1. Coat the fish with the flour.

2. Heat **2 tablespoons** of the oil in a 12-inch skillet over medium-high heat. Add the fish and cook for 8 minutes or until it's browned on both sides and cooked through. Remove the fish and keep it warm.

3. Reduce the heat to medium and add the remaining oil. Add the shallots and cook for 1 minute. Stir the broth, oregano, tomatoes and olives into the skillet. Heat to a boil. Cook for 5 minutes or until the sauce thickens slightly. Season to taste.

4. Prepare the couscous using broth instead of water according to the package directions. Spoon the couscous on a serving platter. Top with the fish. Spoon the sauce mixture over the fish.

Pacific Coast Salmon with Pan-Roasted Corn Salsa

Makes 4 servings

START TO FINISH:
30 minutes

Prepping: 5 minutes
Baking/Cooking:
 25 minutes

4 **fresh salmon fillets (about 1½ pounds)**
1 **jar (16 ounces) Pace® Chunky Salsa**
1 **teaspoon olive oil**
1 **cup frozen whole kernel corn, thawed**
1 **tablespoon chopped fresh cilantro leaves**
1 **tablespoon lemon juice**

1. Arrange the salmon in 17×11-inch roasting pan. Spoon ½ **cup** salsa over the fish.

2. Bake at 400°F. for 15 minutes or until the fish flakes easily when tested with a fork.

3. Heat the oil in an 8-inch nonstick skillet over medium heat. Add the corn and cook for 4 minutes or until the corn starts to brown.

4. Stir the remaining salsa, cilantro and lemon juice into the skillet. Cook until hot. Serve the salmon with the corn salsa.

Shopping for Seafood

• Fresh fish has firm, shiny and elastic flesh. Don't buy fish that is discolored or slimy.

• Fresh fish and shellfish shouldn't smell "fishy."

• Eyes should be bright and clear.

• Scales should be bright, shiny and cling to the skin.

Storing

• Store fish in the refrigerator as soon as possible. As with all flesh foods, fish should be wrapped well so the package can't leak on other foods.

• Raw fish and shellfish should not be thawed at room temperature. Always thaw frozen fish in the refrigerator.

• Defrosted fish should be cooked within two days. Refrigerate if you are not cooking immediately after thawing. When in doubt, throw it out.

Handling

• Always wash hands before and after handling seafood. Use disposable gloves for extra protection.

• Always clean and sanitize any tools, knives, cutting boards, sink and all work surfaces after touching raw seafood. Cross contamination of raw foods with prepared foods is a common culprit of foodborne illness.

Pre-Game Paella

Makes 8 servings

- **1 tablespoon vegetable oil**
- **2 cups uncooked regular long-grain white rice**
- **4 cups Swanson® Chicken Broth (Regular, Natural Goodness™ or Certified Organic), heated**
- **1 cup Pace® Chunky Salsa**
- **1 teaspoon ground turmeric**
- **1 package (16 ounces) turkey kielbasa, sliced**
- **1 package (12 ounces) frozen shelled and deveined small cooked shrimp, thawed (2 cups)**
- **1 package (about 10 ounces) refrigerated cooked chicken breast strips (2 cups)**

1. Heat the oil in a 12-inch skillet over medium heat. Add the rice and cook for 30 seconds, stirring constantly. Stir in the broth, salsa and turmeric and heat to a boil. Reduce the heat to low. Cover and cook for 15 minutes.

2. Stir in the kielbasa, shrimp and chicken. Cover and cook for 5 minutes or until the rice is tender and most of the liquid is absorbed.

**START TO FINISH:
45 minutes**

Prepping: 15 minutes
Cooking: 25 minutes
Standing: 5 minutes

Campbell's Kitchen Tip:
Some like it hot and some don't! Before selecting which salsa to use in this recipe (hot, medium or mild), consider the other foods being served and guests' preference for spicy foods.

Seafood Tomato Alfredo

Makes 4 servings

**START TO FINISH:
25 minutes**

Prepping: 5 minutes
Cooking: 20 minutes

1 tablespoon butter

1 medium onion, chopped (about ½ cup)

1 can (10¾ ounces) Campbell's® Condensed Cream of Mushroom with Roasted Garlic Soup

½ cup milk

1 can (14.5 ounces) diced canned tomatoes, undrained

1 pound fresh fish fillets (flounder, haddock **or** halibut), cut into 2-inch pieces

Hot cooked linguine

1. Heat the butter in a 10-inch skillet over medium heat. Add the onion and cook until it's tender.

2. Stir the soup, milk and tomatoes into the skillet. Heat to a boil. Add the fish to the skillet and reduce the heat to low. Cover and cook for 10 minutes or until the fish flakes easily when tested with a fork.

3. Serve over the linguine.

Tuna & Pasta Cheddar Melt

Makes 4 servings

1 can (10½ ounces) Campbell's® Condensed Chicken Broth

1 soup can water

3 cups **uncooked** corkscrew pasta

1 can (10¾ ounces) Campbell's® Condensed Cream of
　　Mushroom Soup (Regular **or** 98% Fat Free)

1 cup milk

1 can (about 6 ounces) tuna, drained and flaked

1 cup shredded Cheddar cheese (4 ounces)

2 tablespoons Italian-seasoned dry bread crumbs

2 teaspoons butter **or** margarine, melted

**START TO FINISH:
20 minutes**

Prepping/Cooking:
20 minutes

1. Heat the broth and water in a 10-inch skillet over high heat to a boil. Add the pasta. Reduce the heat to medium. Cook until the pasta is tender but still firm, stirring often. Do not drain.

2. Stir the soup, milk and tuna into the skillet. Top with the cheese. Mix the bread crumbs with the butter in a small cup. Sprinkle the crumb mixture over the tuna mixture. Cook until the mixture is hot and bubbling.

Grilling

Firecracker Flank Steak

Makes 8 servings

- 1 jar (16 ounces) Pace® Chunky Salsa
- 2 cups orange juice
- ½ cup olive oil
- 2 tablespoons **each** packed brown sugar, soy sauce **and** Dijon-style mustard
- 1 teaspoon ground ginger
- 2 pounds beef flank steak, 1-inch thick
- Hot cooked rice
- Chopped fresh parsley

1. Stir the salsa, orange juice, oil, sugar, soy, mustard and ginger in a 13×9×2-inch shallow, nonmetallic dish or gallon-size resealable plastic bag. Add the steak and turn it over to coat with the marinade. Cover the dish or seal the plastic bag and refrigerate it for 1 hour or overnight, turning the steak over a few times while it's marinating.

2. Lightly oil the grill rack and heat the grill to medium. Remove the steak from the marinade.

3. Grill the steak for 25 minutes or until desired doneness, turning the steak over halfway through cooking and brushing it often with the marinade while it's cooking.

4. Heat the remaining marinade in a 1-quart saucepan over medium heat to a boil. Reduce the heat to low. Cook for 10 minutes. Thinly slice the steak and serve with the rice and sauce. Sprinkle with parsley.

Tijuana T-Bones

Makes 4 servings

START TO FINISH:
1 hour, 22 minutes

Prepping: 10 minutes
Marinating: 1 hour
Grilling: 12 minutes

1½ cups Pace® Chunky Salsa

2½ teaspoons ground cumin

4 T-bone steaks (about 8 ounces **each**), ½-inch thick

2 tablespoons fresh lime juice

¼ cup chopped fresh cilantro leaves

1 can (about 15 ounces) black beans, rinsed and drained

1 large avocado, peeled, pitted and chopped (about 1½ cups)

1. Stir **1 cup** of the salsa and **2 teaspoons** of the cumin in a 13×9×2-inch shallow, nonmetallic dish or gallon-size resealable plastic bag. Add the steaks and turn them over to coat with the marinade. Cover the dish or seal the plastic bag and refrigerate it for 1 hour, turning the steaks over a few times while they're marinating.

2. Stir the remaining salsa and cumin, lime juice, cilantro, beans and avocado in a small bowl and set aside.

3. Lightly oil the grill rack and heat the grill to medium. Remove the steaks from the marinade. Throw away any remaining marinade.

4. Grill the steaks for 12 minutes for medium-rare* or to desired doneness, turning the steaks over halfway through cooking. Serve the steaks with the salsa mixture.

The internal temperature of the meat should reach 145°F.

Grilled Picante Beef & Vegetable Wraps

Makes 6 sandwiches

- ⅔ **cup mayonnaise**
- ½ **cup Pace® Cilantro Chunky Salsa**
- ⅓ **cup chopped fresh cilantro leaves**
- 1 **tablespoon lime juice**
- ½ **teaspoon ground cumin**
- ¼ **teaspoon crushed red pepper**
- ¼ **teaspoon celery seed**
- 1½ **cups shredded cabbage**
- ⅓ **cup green pepper cut in 2-inch-long strips**
- 1¾ **pounds ground beef**
- 1 **cup Pace® Picante Sauce**
- ¾ **cup crushed corn chips**
- 2 **medium green onions, chopped (about ¼ cup)**
- ¾ **cup shredded pepper Jack cheese**
- 6 **flour tortillas (10-inch)**

**START TO FINISH:
35 minutes**

Prepping: 20 minutes
Grilling: 15 minutes

Grilling

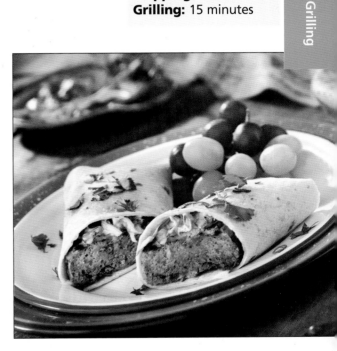

1. Stir the mayonnaise, salsa, cilantro, lime juice, cumin, red pepper and celery seed in a medium bowl. Add the cabbage and green pepper, tossing until well coated. Cover and refrigerate until serving time.

2. Thoroughly mix the beef, picante sauce, chips, green onions and cheese in a medium bowl. Shape the mixture into 6 (7-inch-long and 2-inch wide) burgers.

3. Lightly oil the grill rack and heat the grill to medium. Grill the burgers for 12 minutes for medium* or to desired doneness, turning the burgers over halfway through cooking. Keep warm.

4. Wrap the tortillas in foil. Grill the tortillas for 3 minutes or until they're warm. Put the tortillas on the work surface. Put a burger in the center of each tortilla. Divide the cabbage mixture among the burgers. Roll up each tortilla to enclose the filling. Slice the wrap diagonally in half.

The internal temperature of the burgers should reach 145°F.

Bloody Mary Steak

Makes 6 servings

START TO FINISH:
1 hour, 17 minutes

Prepping: 5 minutes
Marinating: 1 hour
Grilling: 12 minutes

1½ cups V8® Spicy Hot Vegetable Juice
¼ cup prepared horseradish
2 tablespoons lemon juice
2 tablespoons Worcestershire sauce
1½ pounds beef flank **or** boneless sirloin steak, 1-inch thick
Cracked black pepper

1. Stir the vegetable juice, horseradish, lemon juice and Worcestershire sauce in a small bowl. Reserve **1 cup** of the mixture for the sauce.

2. Pour the remaining vegetable juice mixture into a 13×9×2-inch shallow, nonmetallic dish or gallon-size resealable plastic bag. Add the steak and turn it over to coat with the marinade. Cover the dish or seal the plastic bag and refrigerate it for 1 hour or overnight, turning the steak over a few times while it's marinating.

3. Lightly oil the grill rack and heat the grill to medium. Remove the steak from the marinade. Throw away the marinade. Sprinkle the steak with the black pepper.

4. Grill the steak for 12 minutes for medium-rare* or to desired doneness, turning the steak over halfway through cooking.

5. Pour the reserved juice mixture in a 1-quart saucepan. Heat over medium heat to a boil. Reduce the heat to medium-low. Cook for 6 minutes or until the sauce thickens slightly. Thinly slice the steak and serve with the sauce.

The internal temperature of the steak should reach 145°F.

Ginger Peach Barbecued Chicken

Makes 8 servings

2 tablespoons cornstarch
1 can (10½ ounces) Campbell's® Condensed Chicken Broth
½ cup peach preserves
2 tablespoons dry sherry
1 tablespoon soy sauce
½ teaspoon ground ginger
4½ pounds chicken parts

START TO FINISH:
50 minutes

Prepping: 5 minutes
Cooking/Grilling:
45 minutes

1. Stir the cornstarch, broth, preserves, sherry, soy and ginger in a 2-quart saucepan. Cook and stir over high heat until the mixture boils and thickens. Remove from the heat. Reserve **1 cup** of the broth mixture for barbecue sauce.

2. Lightly oil the grill rack and heat the grill to medium. Grill the chicken for 20 minutes, turning the chicken over halfway through cooking. Grill for 20 minutes more or until chicken is cooked through*, turning and brushing it often with the reserved broth mixture while grilling. Serve the chicken with the remaining broth mixture.

*The internal temperature of the chicken should reach 170°F.

Time-Saving Tip:
Barbecue sauce can be made ahead and refrigerated until it's ready to use.

Grilling

Grilled Citrus Chicken with Black Bean Salsa

Makes 6 servings

START TO FINISH:
40 minutes

Prepping: 10 minutes
Marinating:
  20 minutes
Grilling: 10 minutes

3 tablespoons lemon juice

2 tablespoons olive oil

⅓ cup chopped fresh cilantro leaves

2 cloves garlic, minced

¼ teaspoon crushed red pepper

4 to 6 skinless, boneless chicken breast halves

1 jar (16 ounces) Pace® Chunky Salsa

1 can (about 15 ounces) black beans, rinsed and drained

1. Stir **2 tablespoons** of the lemon juice, oil, **3 tablespoons** of the cilantro, garlic and red pepper in a 3-quart nonmetallic, shallow baking dish or gallon-size resealable plastic bag. Add the chicken and turn it over to coat with the marinade. Cover the dish or seal the plastic bag and refrigerate it for 20 minutes turning the chicken over a few times while it's marinating.

2. Stir the remaining lemon juice, cilantro, salsa and beans in a medium bowl and set aside.

3. Lightly oil the grill rack and heat the grill to medium. Remove the chicken from the marinade. Throw away any remaining marinade.

4. Grill the chicken for 10 minutes or until the chicken is cooked through*, turning the chicken over halfway through cooking. Serve the chicken with the salsa mixture.

The internal temperature of the chicken should reach 160°F.

Pork Tenderloin Cubano with Mango Mojo

Makes 6 servings

- 1 whole pork tenderloin (1½ pounds), butterflied
- 1 cup Pace® Chipotle Chunky Salsa
- 7½ ounces cooked chorizo sausage **or** pepperoni, chopped (about 2 cups)
- ½ cup Pepperidge Farm® Garlic Herb Croutons, crushed
- 1 cup orange juice
- 3 tablespoons chopped fresh cilantro leaves
- 2 tablespoons packed brown sugar
- 1 ripe mango, peeled and chopped (about 1½ cups)

START TO FINISH:
1 hour

Prepping: 20 minutes
Cooking/Grilling:
  30 minutes
Standing: 10 minutes

Grilling

1. Put the pork between 2 sheets of plastic wrap. Working from the center, pound the pork flat into a 14×6-inch rectangle. Remove the plastic wrap.

2. Stir ½ **cup** of the salsa, the chorizo and croutons in a small bowl. Spread the chorizo mixture lengthwise down the center of the pork. Fold the sides over the filling to form a 14-inch long roll. Tie the pork crosswise at 2-inch intervals with kitchen twine.

3. Add the remaining salsa, orange juice, cilantro, brown sugar and mango to an electric blender or food processor container. Cover and blend the mixture until it's smooth and pour into a 10-inch skillet. Heat over medium-high heat to a boil. Reduce the heat to medium-low. Cook and stir for 20 minutes or until the sauce thickens.

4. Lightly oil the grill rack and heat the grill to medium. Grill the pork for 20 to 30 minutes or until cooked through but slightly pink*, turning the pork over halfway through cooking. Remove the pork from the grill and let it stand for 10 minutes. Thinly slice the pork and serve with the mango sauce.

The internal temperature of the pork should reach 155°F. During the standing time the temperature will continue to increase to 160°F.

Garlic Pork Kabobs

Makes 4 servings

**START TO FINISH:
40 minutes**

Prepping: 15 minutes
Cooking/Grilling:
25 minutes

Easy Substitution Tip:
Substitute 1¾ cups
Swanson® Chicken
Broth (Regular, Natural
Goodness™ or Certified
Organic) and 2 cloves
garlic, minced, for the
Seasoned Chicken
Broth.

- 2 **tablespoons cornstarch**
- 1¾ **cups Swanson® Seasoned Chicken Broth with Roasted Garlic**
- 1 **tablespoon packed brown sugar**
- 1 **tablespoon ketchup**
- 2 **teaspoons vinegar**
- 1 **pound boneless pork loin, cut into 1-inch cubes**
- 12 **medium mushrooms**
- 1 **large red onion, cut into 12 wedges**
- 4 **cherry tomatoes**
  Hot cooked rice

1. Stir the cornstarch, broth, brown sugar, ketchup and vinegar in a 2-quart saucepan. Cook and stir over high heat until the mixture boils and thickens. Remove from the heat.

2. Thread the pork, mushrooms and red onion alternately onto 4 long skewers.

3. Lightly oil the grill rack and heat the grill to medium. Grill the kabobs for 20 minutes or until the pork is cooked through but slightly pink in the center, turning and brushing the kabobs often with the broth mixture while cooking. Thread a tomato on each skewer.

4. Heat the remaining broth mixture to a boil. Serve with kabobs and rice.

Grilled Fish Steaks with Chunky Tomato Sauce

Makes 6 servings

Vegetable cooking spray

1 stalk celery, chopped (about ½ cup)

1 small green pepper, chopped (about ½ cup)

1 medium onion, chopped (about ½ cup)

½ teaspoon dried thyme leaves, crushed

¼ teaspoon garlic powder **or** 2 cloves garlic, minced

1 can (10¾ ounces) Campbell's® Healthy Request® Condensed Tomato Soup

2 tablespoons lemon juice

⅛ teaspoon hot pepper sauce (optional)

6 fresh halibut steaks, 1-inch thick (about 2¼ pounds)

START TO FINISH:
25 minutes

Prepping: 5 minutes
Cooking/Grilling:
20 minutes

Grilling

1. Spray a 1½-quart saucepan with cooking spray. Heat over medium heat for 1 minute. Add the celery, green pepper, onion, thyme and garlic powder. Cook until the vegetables are tender.

2. Stir the soup, lemon juice and hot pepper sauce, if desired into the saucepan. Heat to a boil. Reduce the heat to low. Cook for 5 minutes.

3. Lightly oil the grill rack and heat the grill to medium. Grill the fish for 10 minutes or until the fish flakes easily when tested with a fork, turning the fish over halfway through cooking. Serve the sauce over the fish.

Grilled Swordfish Steaks with Citrus Salsa

Makes 4 servings

START TO FINISH:
25 minutes

Prepping: 15 minutes
Cooking/Grilling:
  10 minutes

Easy Substitution Tip:
Enjoy a change in taste
when you try this recipe
with tuna or halibut
steaks.

¾ cup Pace® Picante Sauce **or** Chunky Salsa
2 tablespoons orange juice
1 tablespoon chopped fresh cilantro leaves
1 teaspoon grated orange peel
1 cup coarsely chopped orange
1 medium tomato, chopped (about 1 cup)
2 medium green onions, sliced (about ¼ cup)
4 fresh swordfish steaks, 1-inch thick (about 1½ pounds)

1. Stir the picante sauce, orange juice, cilantro and orange peel in a
small bowl. Reserve ½ **cup** and set it aside. Stir the orange, tomato
and green onions into the remaining picante mixture.

2. Lightly oil the grill rack and heat the grill to medium. Grill the fish
for 10 minutes or until the fish flakes easily when tested with a fork,
turning the fish halfway through grilling and brushing often with
reserved picante sauce mixture. Throw away any remaining picante
sauce mixture. Serve the fish with the citrus salsa.

Grilled Bruschetta

Makes 8 servings

3 tablespoons olive oil

2 tablespoons red wine vinegar

2 cloves garlic, minced*

½ teaspoon cracked black pepper

2 tablespoons chopped fresh parsley **or** basil leaves

2 medium tomatoes, chopped (about 2 cups)

1 package (11.25 ounces) Pepperidge Farm® Parmesan **or** Garlic Texas Toast

START TO FINISH:
22 minutes

Prepping: 5 minutes
Marinating:
  15 minutes
Grilling: 2 minutes

1. Stir the oil, vinegar, garlic, black pepper, parsley and tomatoes in a small bowl. Let the mixture stand for at least 15 minutes or until the flavors are blended.

2. Lightly oil the grill rack and heat the grill to medium.

3. Grill the toast slices for 2 minutes or until they're browned and heated through, turning once.

4. Divide the tomato mixture evenly among the toast slices. Serve immediately.

Omit garlic if using garlic Texas toast.

Herb Grilling Sauce

Makes 2 cups

START TO FINISH:
5 minutes

Prepping: 5 minutes

Campbell's Kitchen Tip:
Use **about ½ cup** broth mixture at a time in a separate small bowl for basting raw chicken, fish or pork. Discard any basting mixture left in the small bowl.

1¾ cups Swanson® Chicken Broth (Regular, Natural Goodness™ or Certified Organic)
3 tablespoons lemon juice
1 teaspoon dried basil leaves, crushed
1 teaspoon dried thyme leaves, crushed
⅛ teaspoon ground black pepper

Stir the broth, lemon juice, basil, thyme and black pepper in a small bowl. Use the broth mixture to baste chicken, fish or pork during grilling.

Great Grilling

Whether you're grilling indoors or outdoors, rubs and marinades add flavor and tenderize your favorite meats.

Rubs are a blend of spices, herbs and seasonings used to coat the surface of meat. They can be dry or include just enough liquid, such as oil, that turn them into pastes. The meat is coated with a rub just before grilling or hours in advance and refrigerated. You can buy prepared rubs or easily make them yourself with your favorite herbs, spices, mustard and other ingredients.

Marinades are seasoned, acidic liquids that flavor and tenderize meat. You can buy bottled marinades, or use prepared salad dressings, barbecue sauces, mustards and teriyaki sauces. Or make your own from your favorite herbs and spices, using acidic ingredients such as citrus juices, vinegar (try flavored ones), wine, yogurt or foods that naturally tenderize meat, such as fresh gingerroot, pineapple and papaya juices.

Tips for Marinating

- Figure ¼ to ½ cup marinade for each 1 to 2 pounds of meat.

- Always refrigerate the meat while it's marinating.

- Use a glass dish or plastic bag for marinating. Acidic ingredients in marinades may cause chemical reactions with metal bowls that could give an off-taste to the meat.

- If tenderizing is your goal, marinate 6 hours or overnight. If you're marinating meat to enhance the flavor, marinate at least 15 minutes or as long as 2 hours.

- Never re-use marinades for basting or for sauces served over the meat; prepare additional marinade for that or reserve some before you marinate. Discard marinades immediately after use.

Smart Grilling

- Gas or charcoal? Gas grilling is quicker, neater and fires up faster than charcoal, provides even heat and offers good temperature control, but charcoal gives that distinctive flavor that we all identify as "grilled."

- Preheat the grill. Light your coals about 30 minutes before cooking time, or preheat your gas grill to 350°F. before adding foods.

- Use thermometers to check internal temperatures for doneness. Beef should be 145°F. for medium rare, 160°F. for medium, and 170°F. for well done. Pork should be 160°F. for medium. Poultry, with bone-in, should be 170°F.; boneless should be 160°F.

- You don't really need a lot of equipment, but grilling utensils, such as tongs, long-handled brush and fork, an instant-read thermometer and a wire scraper can make your grilling life easier.

- Keep work surfaces clean and safe. Wipe down work surfaces often. Also, use separate platters and utensils for raw and cooked foods in order to avoid any problems associated with bacterial contamination.

- Be adventurous. Grilling isn't just about meat, fish and chicken. Try grilling vegetables, breads or even fruits for dessert.

Slow Cooking

Orange Chicken with Green Onions and Walnuts

Makes 8 servings

   2 **tablespoons cornstarch**
1½ **cups Swanson® Chicken Broth (Regular, Natural Goodness™
      or Certified Organic)**
   ¼ **cup teriyaki sauce**
   3 **cloves garlic, minced**
   ¾ **cup orange marmalade**
   4 **medium green onions, sliced (about ½ cup)**
   8 **skinless chicken thighs (about 2 pounds)**
   ½ **cup walnut pieces**
      Hot cooked rice

1. Stir the cornstarch, broth, teriyaki sauce, garlic, marmalade and
¼ **cup** green onions in a 6-quart slow cooker. Add the chicken and
turn to coat with the broth mixture.

2. Cover and cook on LOW for 8 to 9 hours* or until the chicken is
cooked through. Sprinkle with walnuts and remaining green onions
before serving. Serve with the rice.

Or on HIGH for 4 to 5 hours

Beef Bourguignonne

Makes 6 servings

START TO FINISH:
8 to 9 hours,
10 minutes

Prepping: 10 minutes
Cooking: 8 to 9 hours

1 can (10¾ ounces) Campbell's® Condensed Golden
    Mushroom Soup
1 cup Burgundy **or** other dry red wine
2 cloves garlic, minced
1 teaspoon dried thyme leaves, crushed
2 cups small button mushrooms (about 6 ounces)
2 cups fresh **or** frozen whole baby carrots
1 cup frozen small whole onions
1½ pounds beef top round steak, 1½-inches thick, cut into
    1-inch pieces

1. Stir the soup, wine, garlic, thyme, mushrooms, carrots, onions and beef in a 3½-quart slow cooker.

2. Cover and cook on LOW for 8 to 9 hours* or until the beef is fork-tender.

Or on HIGH for 4 to 5 hours

Chicken in Creamy Sun-Dried Tomato Sauce

Makes 8 servings

2 cans (10¾ ounces **each**) Campbell's® Condensed Cream of Chicken with Herbs Soup

1 cup Chablis **or** other dry white wine

¼ cup coarsely chopped pitted kalamata **or** oil-cured olives

2 tablespoons drained capers

2 cloves garlic, minced

1 can (14 ounces) artichoke hearts, drained and chopped

1 cup drained, coarsely chopped sun-dried tomatoes

8 skinless, boneless chicken breast halves

½ cup chopped fresh basil leaves (optional)

Hot cooked rice, egg noodles **or** seasoned mashed potatoes

START TO FINISH:
7 to 8 hours,
15 minutes

Prepping: 15 minutes
Cooking: 7 to 8 hours

Easy Substitution Tip:
Substitute Swanson® Chicken Broth (Regular, Natural Goodness™ or Certified Organic) for the wine.

Slow Cooking

1. Stir the soup, wine, olives, capers, garlic, artichokes and tomatoes in a 3½-quart slow cooker. Add the chicken and turn to coat with the soup mixture.

2. Cover and cook on LOW for 7 to 8 hours* or until chicken is cooked through. Sprinkle with basil, if desired. Serve with rice, noodles or potatoes.

Or on HIGH for 4 to 5 hours

Creamy Chicken & Wild Rice

Makes 8 servings

START TO FINISH:
7 to 8 hours,
10 minutes

Prepping: 10 minutes
Cooking: 7 to 8 hours

2 cans (10¾ ounces **each**) Campbell's® Condensed Cream of Chicken Soup (Regular **or** 98% Fat Free)

1½ cups water

4 large carrots, thickly sliced (about 3 cups)

1 package (6 ounces) seasoned long-grain and wild rice mix

8 skinless, boneless chicken breast halves

1. Stir the soup, water, carrots, rice and seasoning packet in a 3½-quart slow cooker. Add the chicken and turn to coat with the soup mixture.

2. Cover and cook on LOW for 7 to 8 hours* or until chicken is cooked through.

Or on HIGH for 4 to 5 hours

Foiled Again

Have you ever cooked a turkey breast or other large roast in your slow cooker and had problems removing it in one piece after it was cooked? Try this: Before putting food in the crock, fold two or three pieces of aluminum foil into strips about 1 to 1½ inches wide. Drape the strips so that the middle sections line the bottom of the crock and the ends hang out of the top of the cooker. Make sure the strips crisscross each other in the bottom of the crock.

Place the food in the cooker on top of the crisscrossed strips. Add any remaining ingredients and put the lid on the cooker so that it sits on the ends of the strips.

When the food is cooked, use the ends of the foil strips to lift the food out of the cooker and onto the serving plate.

Hearty Pork Stew

Makes 8 servings

2 **pounds sweet potatoes, peeled and cut into 2-inch pieces (about 2 cups)**

2 **pounds boneless pork shoulder, cut into 1-inch cubes**

1 **can (14½ ounces) Campbell's® Chicken Gravy**

1 **teaspoon dried thyme leaves, crushed**

½ **teaspoon crushed red pepper**

1 **can (15 ounces) black-eyed peas, rinsed and drained**

START TO FINISH:
7 to 8 hours,
25 minutes

Prepping: 25 minutes
Cooking: 7 to 8 hours

1. Put the potatoes in a 4- to 6-quart slow cooker. Top with the pork.

2. Stir the gravy, thyme, red pepper and peas in a small bowl. Pour over the pork and potatoes.

3. Cover and cook on LOW for 7 to 8 hours* or until the meat is fork-tender.

Or on HIGH for 4 to 5 hours

Slow Cooking

Creamy Blush Sauce with Turkey and Penne

Makes 8 servings

START TO FINISH:
7 to 8 hours,
10 minutes

Prepping: 10 minutes
Cooking: 7 to 8 hours

4 turkey thighs, skin removed (about 3 pounds)

1 jar (1 pound 9.75 ounces) Prego® Chunky Garden Mushroom & Green Pepper Italian Sauce

½ teaspoon crushed red pepper

½ cup half-and-half

Hot cooked tube-shaped pasta (penne)

Grated Parmesan cheese

1. Put the turkey in a 3½- to 5-quart slow cooker. Pour the Italian sauce over the turkey and sprinkle with pepper.

2. Cover and cook on LOW for 7 to 8 hours* or until turkey is fork-tender and cooked through. Remove the turkey from the cooker. Remove the turkey meat from the bones and cut it into cubes.

3. Stir the turkey meat and the half-and-half into the cooker. Cover and cook for 10 minutes or until hot. Spoon sauce and turkey over the pasta. Sprinkle with cheese.

Or on HIGH for 4 to 5 hours

Golden Mushroom Pork & Apples

Makes 8 servings

2 cans (10¾ ounces **each**) Campbell's® Condensed Golden
   Mushroom Soup

½ cup water

1 tablespoon packed brown sugar

1 tablespoon Worcestershire sauce

1 teaspoon dried thyme leaves, crushed

8 boneless pork chops, ¾-inch thick (about 2 pounds)

4 large Granny Smith apples, sliced

2 large onions, sliced (about 2 cups)

START TO FINISH:
8 to 9 hours,
10 minutes

Prepping: 10 minutes
Cooking: 8 to 9 hours

1. Stir the soup, water, brown sugar, Worcestershire and thyme in a 3½-quart slow cooker. Add the pork and turn to coat with the soup mixture. Top with the apples and onions.

2. Cover and cook on LOW for 8 to 9 hours* or until the pork is cooked through.

Or on HIGH for 4 to 5 hours

Slow Cooking

Apricot Glazed Pork Roast

Makes 8 servings

START TO FINISH:
8 to 9 hours,
15 minutes

Prepping: 5 minutes
Cooking: 8 to 9 hours
Standing: 10 minutes

Campbell's Kitchen Tip:

For thicker sauce, stir
2 tablespoons
cornstarch and
2 tablespoons water in a
small cup. Remove the
roast from the cooker.
Stir the cornstarch
mixture into cooker.
Turn heat to HIGH.
Cover and cook for
10 minutes or until
the mixture boils and
thickens.

1 can (10½ ounces) Campbell's® Condensed Chicken Broth
1 jar (18 ounces) apricot preserves
2 tablespoons Dijon-style mustard
1 large onion, chopped (about 1 cup)
   3½- to 4-pound boneless pork loin

1. Stir the broth, preserves, mustard and onion in a 3½-quart slow cooker. Cut the pork to fit. Add the pork to cooker and turn to coat with the broth mixture.

2. Cover and cook on LOW for 8 to 9 hours* or until the meat is fork-tender.

3. Remove the roast from the cooker to a cutting board and let it stand for 10 minutes. Thinly slice the roast and arrange on a serving platter. Pour the juices from the cooker into a gravy boat and serve with the roast.

Or on HIGH for 4 to 5 hours

Slow-Cooked Autumn Brisket

Makes 8 servings

3-pound boneless beef brisket
1 small head cabbage (about 1 pound), cut into 8 wedges
1 large sweet potato (about ¾ pound), peeled and cut into 1-inch pieces
1 large onion, cut into 8 wedges
1 medium Granny Smith apple, cored and cut into 8 wedges
2 cans (10¾ ounces **each**) Campbell's® Condensed Cream of Celery Soup (Regular **or** 98% Fat Free)
1 cup water
2 teaspoons caraway seed (optional)

START TO FINISH:
8 to 9 hours, 30 minutes

Prepping: 20 minutes
Cooking: 8 to 9 hours
Standing: 10 minutes

1. Season brisket if desired.

2. Put the brisket in a 6-quart slow cooker. Top with the cabbage, sweet potato, onion and apple.

3. Stir the soup, water and caraway, if desired, in a medium bowl. Pour the soup mixture over the brisket and vegetable mixture.

4. Cover and cook on LOW for 8 to 9 hours* or until the meat is fork-tender.

5. Remove the brisket from the cooker to a cutting board and let it stand for 10 minutes. Thinly slice brisket across the grain. Arrange brisket on a serving platter. Remove the vegetables and fruit with a slotted spoon and put on platter. Pour the pan juices into a gravy boat and serve with the brisket.

*Or on HIGH for 4 to 5 hours

Slow Cooking

Weekday Pot Roast & Vegetables

Makes 6 to 8 servings

START TO FINISH:
10 to 12 hours,
25 minutes

Prepping: 15 minutes
Cooking:
   10 to 12 hours
Standing: 10 minutes

2- to 2½-pound boneless beef bottom round **or** chuck pot roast

1 teaspoon garlic powder

1 tablespoon vegetable oil

4 medium potatoes (about 1 pound), each cut into 6 wedges

3 cups fresh **or** frozen baby carrots

1 medium onion, thickly sliced (about ¾ cup)

2 teaspoons dried basil leaves, crushed

2 cans (10¼ ounces **each**) Campbell's® Beef Gravy

1. Season the roast with garlic powder. Heat the oil in a 10-inch skillet over medium-high heat. Add the roast and cook until it's browned on all sides.

2. Stir the potatoes, carrots, onion and basil in a 3½-quart slow cooker. Top with the roast. Pour the gravy over the roast and vegetables.

3. Cover and cook on LOW for 10 to 12 hours* or until the meat is fork-tender.

4. Remove the roast from the cooker to a cutting board and let it stand for 10 minutes. Thinly slice the roast and arrange on a serving platter. Remove the vegetables with a slotted spoon and put on platter. Pour the juices from the cooker into a gravy boat and serve with the roast and vegetables.

*Or on HIGH for 5 to 6 hours

Zesty Slow-Cooker Italian Pot Roast

Makes 4 to 6 servings

2½-pound boneless beef bottom round **or** chuck pot roast

½ teaspoon ground black pepper

4 medium potatoes, (about 1 pound), cut into quarters

2 cups fresh **or** frozen whole baby carrots

1 stalk celery, cut into 1-inch pieces

1 medium Italian plum tomato, diced

1 can (10¾ ounces) Campbell's® Condensed Tomato Soup

½ cup water

1 tablespoon chopped roasted garlic* **or** fresh garlic

1 teaspoon **each** dried basil leaves, dried oregano leaves **and** dried parsley flakes, crushed

1 teaspoon vinegar

START TO FINISH:
10 to 12 hours,
45 minutes

Prepping: 45 minutes
Cooking:
 10 to 12 hours

1. Season the roast with the black pepper.

2. Put the potatoes, carrots, celery and tomato in a 3½-quart slow cooker.

3. Stir the soup, water, garlic, basil, oregano, parsley flakes and vinegar in a medium bowl. Pour the soup mixture over the roast and vegetables.

4. Cover and cook on LOW for 10 to 12 hours** or until meat is fork-tender.

5. Remove the roast from the cooker to a cutting board and let it stand for 10 minutes. Thinly slice the roast and arrange on a serving platter. Remove the vegetables with a slotted spoon and put on platter. Pour the juices from the cooker into a gravy boat and serve with the roast and vegetables.

To roast garlic, place whole garlic bulb on piece of aluminum foil. Drizzle with vegetable oil and wrap. Roast at 350°F. for 45 minutes or until soft. Peel and chop garlic.

**Or on HIGH 5 to 6 hours*

Campbell's Kitchen Tip:
For thicker gravy, mix ¼ cup all-purpose flour and ½ cup water. Remove roast from the cooker. Stir flour mixture into cooker. Turn heat to HIGH. Cover and cook for 10 minutes or until mixture boils and thickens.

Slow Cooking

Melt-in-Your-Mouth Short Ribs

Makes 6 servings

START TO FINISH:
8 to 10 hours,
10 minutes

Prepping: 10 minutes
Cooking: 8 to 10 hours

3 pounds beef short ribs, cut into individual pieces

2 tablespoons packed brown sugar

3 cloves garlic, minced

1 teaspoon dried thyme leaves, crushed

¼ cup all-purpose flour

1 can (10½ ounces) Campbell's® Condensed French Onion Soup

1 bottle (12 fluid ounces) dark ale **or** beer

Hot mashed potatoes **or** buttered noodles

1. Put the ribs, brown sugar, garlic and thyme in a 3½- to 6-quart slow cooker. Sprinkle with the flour and toss to coat.

2. Stir the soup and ale in a small bowl. Pour soup mixture over the ribs.

3. Cover and cook on LOW for 8 to 10 hours* or until the meat is fork-tender. Remove ribs with a fork or kitchen tongs from the sauce. Spoon off any fat from the sauce before serving. Serve with potatoes or noodles.

Or on HIGH for 4 to 5 hours

Slow-Cooked Pulled Pork Sandwiches

Makes 12 sandwiches

1 tablespoon vegetable oil

3½- to 4-pound boneless pork shoulder roast, netted **or** tied

1 can (10½ ounces) Campbell's® Condensed French Onion Soup

1 cup ketchup

¼ cup cider vinegar

3 tablespoons packed brown sugar

12 round sandwich rolls, split

START TO FINISH:
8 to 10 hours,
25 minutes

Prepping: 15 minutes
Cooking: 8 to 10 hours
Standing: 10 minutes

1. Heat the oil in a 10-inch skillet over medium-high heat. Add the roast and cook until it's well browned on all sides.

2. Stir the soup, ketchup, vinegar and brown sugar in a 5-quart slow cooker. Add the roast and turn to coat with the soup mixture.

3. Cover and cook on LOW for 8 to 10 hours* or until the meat is fork-tender.

4. Remove the roast from the cooker to a cutting board and let it stand for 10 minutes. Using 2 forks, shred the pork. Return the shredded pork to the cooker.

5. Divide the pork and sauce mixture among the rolls.

Or on HIGH for 4 to 5 hours

Slow Cooking

Jambalaya

Makes 6 servings

START TO FINISH:
7 to 8 hours,
55 minutes

Prepping: 15 minutes
Cooking: 7 to 8 hours,
40 minutes

2 cups Swanson® Chicken Broth (Regular, Natural Goodness™ **or** Certified Organic)

1 tablespoon Creole seasoning

1 large green pepper, diced (about 1⅓ cups)

1 large onion, diced (about 1 cup)

2 stalks celery, chopped (about 1 cup)

1 can (about 14½ ounces) diced tomatoes, undrained

1 pound kielbasa, diced

¾ pound skinless, boneless chicken thighs, cut into cubes

1 cup **uncooked** regular long-grain white rice

½ pound fresh medium shrimp, shelled and deveined

1. Stir the broth, Creole seasoning, pepper, onion, celery, tomatoes, kielbasa, chicken and rice in a 3½- to 6-quart slow cooker.

2. Cover and cook on LOW for 7 to 8 hours*.

3. Stir in the shrimp. Cover and cook for 40 minutes more or until chicken is cooked through and shrimp turn pink.

Or on HIGH for 4 to 5 hours

Veal Stew with Garden Vegetables

Makes 6 servings

2- to 2½-pounds veal for stew, cut into 1-inch pieces
Ground black pepper
2 tablespoons olive oil
1 bag (16 ounces) fresh **or** frozen whole baby carrots (about 2½ cups)
1 large onion, diced (about 1 cup)
4 cloves garlic, minced
¼ cup all-purpose flour
2 cups Swanson® Chicken Broth (Regular, Natural Goodness™ **or** Certified Organic)
½ teaspoon dried rosemary leaves, crushed
1 can (14½ ounces) diced tomatoes
1 cup frozen peas
Hot cooked rice **or** barley

**START TO FINISH:
8 to 10 hours,
10 minutes**

Prepping: 10 minutes
Cooking: 8 to 10 hours

Easy Substitution Tip:
Substitute skinless, boneless chicken thighs, cut into 1-inch pieces for the veal.

Slow Cooking

1. Season the veal with the black pepper.

2. Heat the oil in a 4-quart saucepot. Add the veal in 2 batches and cook until it's well browned, stirring often. Remove the veal with a slotted spoon and put it in a 3½- to 6-quart slow cooker.

3. Add the carrots, onion and garlic. Sprinkle with the flour and toss to coat.

4. Stir the broth, rosemary and tomatoes into the cooker.

5. Cover and cook on LOW for 7 to 8 hours*.

6. Stir in the peas. Cover and cook for 1 hour more or until meat is fork-tender. Serve over the rice or barley.

Or on HIGH for 4 to 5 hours

Casseroles and One-Dish Meals

START TO FINISH:
32 minutes

Prepping: 10 minutes
Baking: 22 minutes

Easy Substitution Tip:
Substitute your family's favorite frozen vegetable for the peas.

Tuna Noodle Casserole

Makes 4 servings

1 can (10¾ ounces) Campbell's® Condensed Cream of Mushroom Soup (Regular **or** 98% Fat Free)
½ cup milk
1 cup frozen peas
2 cans (about 6 ounces each) tuna, drained and flaked
2 cups hot cooked medium egg noodles
½ cup shredded Cheddar cheese

1. Preheat oven to 400°F. Stir the soup, milk, peas, tuna and noodles in a 1½-quart casserole.

2. Bake for 20 minutes or until hot. Stir.

3. Sprinkle cheese over the tuna mixture. Bake for 2 minutes more or until the cheese melts.

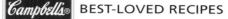

Baked Chicken & Cheese Risotto

Makes 4 servings

START TO FINISH:
1 hour

Prepping: 10 minutes
Baking: 45 minutes
Standing: 5 minutes

1 can (10¾ ounces) Campbell's® Condensed Cream of Mushroom Soup (Regular **or** 98% Fat Free)

1¼ cups water

½ cup milk

1½ cups frozen mixed vegetables

½ pound skinless, boneless chicken breasts, cut into cubes

¼ cup shredded part-skim mozzarella cheese

3 tablespoons grated Parmesan cheese

¾ cup **uncooked** Arborio **or** regular long-grain white rice

1. Stir the soup, water, milk, vegetables, chicken, cheeses and rice in a 13×9×2-inch shallow baking dish. Cover the dish with foil.

2. Bake at 400°F. for 35 minutes. Uncover the dish and stir.

3. Bake for 10 minutes more or until hot and the rice is tender. Let the risotto stand for 5 minutes before serving.

Smoked Turkey & Broccoli Gratin

Makes 4 servings

1 can (10¾ ounces) Campbell's® Condensed Cheddar Cheese Soup

½ cup milk

1 tablespoon Dijon-style mustard

1 package (20 ounces) frozen chopped broccoli, thawed and drained (4 cups)

1 pound cooked smoked turkey, cubed (about 3 cups)

1 cup small shell pasta, cooked and drained

2 tablespoons dry bread crumbs

1 tablespoon butter, melted

**START TO FINISH:
35 minutes**

Prepping: 5 minutes
Baking: 30 minutes

1. Stir the soup, milk, mustard, broccoli, turkey and pasta in a 12×8×2-inch shallow baking dish. Mix the bread crumbs with the butter in a small cup. Sprinkle the bread crumb mixture over the turkey mixture.

2. Bake at 375°F. for 30 minutes or until hot and bubbly.

Casseroles and
One-Dish Meals

Turkey and Stuffing Casserole

Makes 6 servings

**START TO FINISH:
30 minutes**

Prepping: 5 minutes
Baking: 25 minutes

Campbell's Kitchen Tip:
If you don't have any
leftover turkey or
chicken for this recipe,
substitute 1 can
(9.75 ounces) Swanson®
Premium White Chunk
Chicken Breast,
drained.

Vegetable cooking spray
1 can (10¾ ounces) Campbell's® Condensed Cream of
    Mushroom Soup (Regular **or** 98% Fat Free)
1 cup milk **or** water
1 bag (16 ounces) frozen vegetable combination (broccoli,
    cauliflower, carrots), thawed
2 cups cubed cooked turkey **or** chicken
4 cups Pepperidge Farm® Cubed Herb Seasoned Stuffing
1 cup shredded Swiss or Cheddar cheese (4 ounces)

1. Spray a 12×8×2-inch shallow baking dish with cooking spray and
set aside.

2. Stir the soup and milk in a large bowl. Stir in the vegetables, turkey
and stuffing. Spoon the mixture into the prepared dish.

3. Bake at 400°F. for 20 minutes or until hot and bubbly. Stir.

4. Sprinkle the cheese over the turkey mixture. Bake for 5 minutes
more or until the cheese melts.

Turkey Apple Cranberry Bake

Makes 4 servings

1 cup Pepperidge Farm® Herb Seasoned Stuffing

1 tablespoon butter, melted

1 can (10¾ ounces) Campbell's® Condensed Cream of Celery Soup (Regular **or** 98% Fat Free)

½ cup milk

2 cups cubed cooked turkey

1 medium apple, diced (about 1½ cups)

1 stalk celery, finely chopped (about ½ cup)

½ cup dried cranberries

½ cup pecan halves, chopped

START TO FINISH:
50 minutes

Prepping: 20 minutes
Baking: 30 minutes

1. Stir the stuffing and butter in a small bowl. Set aside.

2. Stir the soup, milk, turkey, apple, celery, cranberries and pecans in a 12×8×2-inch shallow baking dish. Sprinkle the reserved stuffing mixture over the turkey mixture.

3. Bake at 400°F. for 30 minutes or until hot and bubbly.

Casseroles and
One-Dish Meals

Garlic Mashed Potatoes & Beef Bake

Makes 4 servings

1 **pound ground beef or ground turkey**

1 **can (10¾ ounces) Campbell's® Condensed Cream of
   Mushroom with Roasted Garlic Soup**

1 **tablespoon Worcestershire sauce**

1 **bag (16 ounces) frozen vegetable combination (broccoli,
   cauliflower, carrots), thawed**

2 **cups water**

3 **tablespoons butter**

¾ **cup milk**

2 **cups instant potato flakes or buds**

1. Cook the beef in a 10-inch skillet over medium-high heat until the
beef is well browned, stirring frequently to break up meat. Pour off
any fat.

2. Stir the beef,
½ **can** soup,
Worcestershire and
vegetables in a
12×8×2-inch
shallow baking
dish.

3. Heat the water,
butter and
remaining soup in a
2-quart saucepan
over high heat to a
boil. Remove from
the heat. Stir in the
milk. Slowly stir in
the potatoes. Spoon
potatoes over the
beef mixture.

4. Bake at 400°F.
for 20 minutes or
until hot.

Beef & Rice Taco Casserole

Makes 4 servings

1 **pound ground beef**
1 **can (10¾ ounces) Campbell's® Condensed Tomato Soup**
1 **cup Pace® Chunky Salsa or Picante Sauce**
½ **cup milk**
½ **cup uncooked instant white rice**
½ **cup crushed tortilla chips**
½ **cup shredded Cheddar cheese**

**START TO FINISH:
35 minutes**

Prepping: 10 minutes
Baking: 25 minutes

1. Cook the beef in a 10-inch skillet over medium-high heat until the beef is well browned, stirring frequently to break up meat. Pour off any fat.

2. Stir the soup, salsa, milk and rice into the skillet. Spoon the soup mixture into a 1½-quart casserole. Cover the dish with foil.

3. Bake at 400°F. for 25 minutes or until hot. Stir.

4. Sprinkle the chips around the edge of the casserole. Sprinkle with the cheese.

Casseroles and
One-Dish Meals

Chicken Florentine Lasagna

Makes 6 servings

START TO FINISH:
1 hour, 15 minutes

Prepping: 10 minutes
Baking: 1 hour
Standing: 5 minutes

Time-Saving Tip:
To thaw spinach, microwave on HIGH for 3 minutes, breaking apart with a fork halfway through heating.

2 cans (10¾ ounces **each**) Campbell's® Condensed Cream of Chicken with Herbs Soup

2 cups milk

1 egg

1 container (15 ounces) ricotta cheese

6 **uncooked** lasagna noodles

1 package (about 10 ounces) frozen chopped spinach, thawed and well drained

2 cups cubed cooked chicken **or** turkey

2 cups shredded Cheddar cheese (8 ounces)

1. Stir the soup and milk in a medium bowl.

2. Stir the egg and ricotta cheese in a small bowl.

3. Spread **1 cup** of the soup mixture in a 13×9×2-inch shallow baking dish. Top with **3** noodles, the ricotta mixture, spinach, chicken, **1 cup** of the Cheddar cheese and **1 cup** of the soup mixture. Top with remaining **3** noodles and remaining soup mixture. Cover the dish with foil.

4. Bake at 375°F. for 1 hour. Uncover the dish and sprinkle with the remaining Cheddar cheese. Let the lasagna stand for 5 minutes before serving.

Easy Chicken Pot Pie

Makes 4 servings

1 can (10¾ ounces) Campbell's® Condensed Cream of Potato Soup

¾ cup milk

⅛ teaspoon ground black pepper

1 cup frozen mixed vegetables, thawed

2 cans (4.5 ounces **each**) Swanson® Premium Chunk Chicken Breast, drained

1 cup all-purpose baking mix

1 egg

START TO FINISH: 35 minutes

Prepping: 5 minutes
Baking: 30 minutes

1. Heat the oven to 400°F.

2. Stir the soup, ¼ **cup** milk, black pepper, vegetables and chicken in a 9-inch pie plate.

3. Stir together the baking mix, egg and the remaining milk with a fork in a small bowl until the ingredients are mixed. Spoon over the chicken mixture.

4. Bake for 30 minutes or until hot and topping is golden.

Shrimp Stuffing au Gratin

Makes 6 servings

START TO FINISH:
45 minutes

Prepping/Cooking:
15 minutes
Baking: 30 minutes

Campbell's Kitchen Tip:
You'll need to purchase 1 pound of fresh medium shrimp to have enough for 2 cups of cooked shrimp needed for this recipe. Heat 4 cups water in a 2-quart saucepan over high heat to a boil. Add the shrimp and cook for 1 to 3 minutes or until the shrimp turn pink. Drain in a colander and rinse under cold water. Remove the shells and devein the shrimp.

4½ cups Pepperidge Farm® Herb Seasoned Stuffing
3 tablespoons butter, melted
1¼ cups water
2 cups cooked broccoli flowerets
2 cups cooked medium shrimp
1 can (10¾ ounces) Campbell's® Condensed Cream of Mushroom Soup (Regular **or** 98% Fat Free)
½ cup milk
2 tablespoons diced pimiento (optional)
1 cup shredded Swiss cheese (4 ounces)

1. Coarsely crush ½ cup of the stuffing. Mix the stuffing and 1 **tablespoon** of the butter in a small cup. Set aside.

2. Stir the water and remaining butter in 12×8×2-inch shallow baking dish. Add the remaining stuffing and stir lightly to coat.

3. Arrange the broccoli and shrimp over the stuffing.

4. Stir the soup, milk, pimiento, if desired and cheese in a small bowl. Pour the soup mixture over the shrimp mixture. Sprinkle with the reserved stuffing mixture.

5. Bake at 350°F. for 30 minutes or until hot.

Easy Chicken & Biscuits

Makes 5 servings

1 can (10¾ ounces) Campbell's® Condensed Cream of Celery Soup (Regular **or** 98% Fat Free)

1 can (10¾ ounces) Campbell's® Condensed Cream of Potato Soup

1 cup milk

¼ teaspoon dried thyme leaves, crushed

¼ teaspoon ground black pepper

4 cups cooked cut-up vegetables*

2 cups cubed cooked chicken

1 package (about 7 ounces) refrigerated buttermilk biscuits (10)

START TO FINISH: 40 minutes

Prepping: 10 minutes
Baking: 30 minutes

1. Stir the soups, milk, thyme, black pepper, vegetables and chicken in a 13×9×2-inch shallow baking dish.

2. Bake at 400°F. for 15 minutes. Stir.

3. Cut each biscuit into quarters. Arrange cut biscuits over the chicken mixture.

4. Bake for 15 minutes more or until the biscuits are golden.

Use a combination of broccoli flowerets, cauliflower flowerets and carrots.

Casseroles and One-Dish Meals

Asian Chicken & Rice Bake

Makes 6 servings

START TO FINISH:
50 minutes

Prepping: 5 minutes
Baking: 45 minutes

Make Ahead Tip:
Prepare recipe through
step 2 and refrigerate.
Remove from
refrigerator and let
stand 15 minutes. Bake
as directed in step 3.

¾ cup **uncooked** regular long-grain white rice
4 to 6 skinless, boneless chicken breast halves
1 can (10¾ ounces) Campbell's® Condensed Golden
   Mushroom Soup
¾ cup water
2 tablespoons soy sauce
2 tablespoons cider vinegar
2 tablespoons honey
1 teaspoon garlic powder
   Paprika

1. Spread the rice in a 12×8×2-inch shallow baking dish. Top with
the chicken.

2. Stir the soup, water, soy, vinegar, honey and garlic powder in a
medium bowl. Pour the soup mixture over the chicken. Sprinkle with
paprika. Cover the dish with foil.

3. Bake at 375°F. for 45 minutes or until the chicken is cooked
through*.

The internal temperature of the chicken should reach 160°F.

Chicken Verde Casserole

Makes 8 servings

Vegetable cooking spray

2 cans (10¾ ounces **each**) Campbell's® Condensed Creamy
   Chicken Verde Soup

1½ cups milk

1 medium onion, chopped (about ½ cup)

10 corn tortillas (6-inch), cut into 1-inch squares

4 cups cubed cooked chicken

1 medium tomato, chopped (about 1 cup)

1 cup shredded Mexican cheese blend (4 ounces)

2 medium green onions, sliced (about ¼ cup)

START TO FINISH:
3 hours,
15 minutes

Prepping: 20 minutes
Refrigerating: 2 hours
Baking: 45 minutes
Standing: 10 minutes

Time-Saving Tip:
Use store-purchased
rotisserie chicken or
refrigerated cooked
chicken strips for the
cubed cooked chicken.

1. Spray a 13×9×2-inch shallow baking dish with cooking spray.

2. Stir the soup, milk and onion in a medium bowl. Spread **1 cup** of
the soup mixture in the prepared dish.

3. Layer ⅓ of the tortillas,
⅓ of the remaining soup
mixture, **2 cups** of the
chicken and ½ cup of the
tomatoes. Repeat the layers.
Top with remaining tortillas,
soup mixture and the
cheese. Cover the dish with
plastic wrap. Refrigerate for
at least 2 hours or overnight.

4. Uncover the dish. Bake at
350°F. for 45 minutes or
until hot. Sprinkle with the
green onions. Let the
casserole stand for
10 minutes before serving.

Gumbo Casserole

Makes 4 servings

START TO FINISH:
40 minutes

Prepping: 5 minutes
Baking: 35 minutes

2 cans (10¾ ounces **each**) Campbell's® Condensed Chicken
   Gumbo Soup

1 soup can water

1 teaspoon dried minced onion

½ teaspoon Cajun seasoning

½ teaspoon garlic powder

1 cup frozen okra, thawed

¾ cup **uncooked** instant white rice

½ pound cooked ham, diced (about 1½ cups)

½ pound cooked shrimp, peeled and deveined

1. Stir the soup, water, onion, Cajun seasoning, garlic powder, okra, rice, ham and shrimp in a 2-quart casserole.

2. Bake at 375°F. for 35 minutes or until hot. Stir before serving. Serve in bowls.

Sausage, Beef & Bean Casserole

Makes 6 servings

- **1 pound sweet Italian pork sausage, cut into 1-inch pieces**
- **½ pound ground beef**
- **1 small onion, chopped (about ¼ cup)**
- **1 bag (6 ounces) baby spinach leaves, washed**
- **1 can (10¾ ounces) Campbell's® Condensed Cream of Mushroom Soup (Regular or 98% Fat Free)**
- **¼ cup milk**
- **1 can (about 15 ounces) white kidney (cannellini) beans, rinsed and drained**
- **1 cup Pepperidge Farm® Herb Seasoned Stuffing**
- **½ cup crumbled blue cheese or shredded Cheddar cheese**

**START TO FINISH:
40 minutes**

Prepping: 10 minutes
Baking: 30 minutes

1. Cook the sausage, beef and onion in a 12-inch nonstick skillet or 5-quart saucepot until the meats are well browned, stirring frequently to break up meat. Pour off fat. Add the spinach and cook until the spinach wilts.

2. Stir the soup, milk and beans into the skillet. Spoon the mixture into a 2-quart casserole.

3. Stir the stuffing and cheese in a small bowl. Sprinkle around the edge of the dish.

4. Bake at 350°F. for 30 minutes or until hot and bubbly and the internal temperature of the sausage mixture is 160°F.

Casseroles and
One-Dish Meals

Unstuffed Pork Chops

Makes 6 servings

START TO FINISH:
40 minutes

Prepping: 10 minutes
Cooking/Baking:
30 minutes

6 **bone-in loin pork chops (¾-inch thick)**
¼ **teaspoon ground black pepper**
1 **tablespoon vegetable oil**
1 **can (10½ ounces) Campbell's® Condensed Chicken Broth**
4 **tablespoons butter**
2 **stalks celery, chopped (about 1 cup)**
1 **medium onion, chopped (about ½ cup)**
4 **cups Pepperidge Farm® Herb Seasoned Stuffing**

1. Season the pork chops with black pepper. Heat the oil in a 12-inch skillet over medium-high heat. Add the pork chops and cook until the chops are well browned on both sides.

2. Heat the broth and butter in a 3-quart saucepan over medium-high heat to a boil. Add the celery and onion and cook for 2 minutes or until the vegetables are tender. Add the stuffing and stir lightly to coat. Spoon the stuffing mixture into a 13×9×2-inch shallow baking dish. Top with the pork chops.

3. Bake at 400°F. for 20 minutes or until the chops are cooked through but slightly pink in center* and the stuffing reaches 165°F.

*The internal temperature of the pork should reach 160°F.

Top It Off!

Casseroles are best when they're topped off. Try any of these toppings:

- Homemade breadcrumbs. A great way to use up day-old bread is to make your own breadcrumbs. For dry breadcrumbs, preheat your oven to 300°F. Place a single layer of bread slices on a baking sheet; bake 5 to 8 minutes or until they're completely dry and lightly browned. Cool completely. Process in a food processor or crush or crumble in a plastic food storage bag until crumbs are very fine. Season with black pepper, garlic powder, dried herbs or spices or grated cheese, as desired.

To make fresh breadcrumbs, process untoasted bread in a food processor and process until crumbs are fine. Season as desired.

- Toasted almonds or walnuts. You'll love the nutty flavor they add to your dish.

- Dried fruits or vegetables. Try some dried cranberries, raisins, even cherries or maybe some chopped bell peppers or shredded carrots.

- Cheese. Shredded varieties, including Cheddar, Swiss and mozzarella, will top off your dish with lots of flavor.

- Crunchy chips or cereal. Crushed or crumbled potato chips, tortilla chips, French fried onions and unsweetened cereals can add a flavorful crunch to your favorite dish.

Pasta and Rice

START TO FINISH:
40 minutes

Prepping: 20 minutes
Baking: 20 minutes

Easy Substitution Tip:
Use 2 cups of your
favorite shredded
cheese for the 8-ounce
package.

3-Cheese Pasta Bake

Makes 4 servings

1 can (10¾ ounces) Campbell's® Condensed Cream of
  Mushroom Soup (Regular **or** 98% Fat Free)

1 package (8 ounces) shredded two-cheese blend

⅓ cup grated Parmesan cheese

1 cup milk

¼ teaspoon ground black pepper

3 cups corkscrew-shaped pasta, cooked and drained

1. Stir the soup, cheeses, milk and black pepper in a 1½-quart
casserole. Stir in the pasta.

2. Bake at 400°F. for 20 minutes or until hot.

Baked Ziti

Makes 4 servings

START TO FINISH:
55 minutes

Prepping: 25 minutes
Baking: 30 minutes

1 jar (1 pound 10 ounces) Prego® Traditional Italian Sauce
1½ cups shredded mozzarella cheese (6 ounces)
3½ cups medium tube-shaped pasta (ziti), cooked and drained
¼ cup grated Parmesan cheese

1. Stir the Italian sauce, **1 cup** mozzarella cheese and pasta in a 12×8×2-inch shallow baking dish. Sprinkle with the remaining mozzarella cheese and Parmesan cheese.

2. Bake at 350°F. for 30 minutes or until hot.

Make Ahead Tip:

To freeze, prepare ziti but do not bake. Cover tightly with foil and freeze. Bake frozen ziti uncovered in a 350°F. oven for 1 hour or until hot. Or, refrigerate frozen ziti for 4 hours to thaw. Bake thawed ziti uncovered at 350°F. for 45 minutes or until hot.

Perfect Pasta...Really Great Rice

● If you're like most cooks, you probably don't measure the water before you cook pasta. But the right amount of water can prevent pasta from sticking while it cooks. Allow 4 cups of water for every 4 ounces of pasta. After adding the pasta to the boiling water, allow the water to return to a boil before you begin clocking the cooking time.

● Salt isn't necessary, but it does add flavor. Figure ¼ teaspoon for every 4 ounces of pasta.

● Immediately drain the pasta to prevent overcooking. It's not necessary to rinse with cold water, unless it's going to be used in a cold pasta salad.

● Properly cooked pasta should be al dente, or tender but firm to the bite, especially if you're going to use it in pasta salad, or in a casserole that will be baked after the pasta has been cooked.

● Different rice varieties require slightly different amounts of liquid and cook times. Check package directions. In general, though, regular medium-grain white rice (not instant or converted) needs about 2 cups of water per cup of rice; brown rice can require up to 3 cups water. Substitute Swanson® Chicken, Beef or Vegetable broth for added flavor.

● Rinse rice before cooking only if package directions indicate to do so.

● There's no need to stir rice while it's cooking unless your recipe says to do so. Stirring generally makes rice sticky and starchy. The primary exception to this rule is Arborio rice, the type used for risotto, which needs to be stirred frequently for the proper texture; again, follow your recipe.

● To test for doneness, bite into a grain or squeeze a grain between your thumb and index finger. The rice is done when it is tender and the center is no longer hard.

Broccoli and Pasta Bianco

Makes 8 servings

1 **package (16 ounces) medium tube-shaped pasta (penne)**
4 **cups fresh or frozen broccoli flowerets**
1 **can (10¾ ounces) Campbell's® Condensed Cream of Mushroom Soup (Regular or 98% Fat Free)**
1½ **cups milk**
½ **teaspoon ground black pepper**
1½ **cups shredded mozzarella cheese (6 ounces)**
¼ **cup shredded Parmesan cheese**

START TO FINISH:
45 minutes

Prepping: 20 minutes
Baking: 25 minutes

1. Prepare the pasta according to the package directions. Add the broccoli during the last 4 minutes of the cooking time. Drain the pasta and broccoli well in a colander.

2. Stir the soup, milk and black pepper in a 12×8×2-inch shallow baking dish. Stir in the pasta mixture, ¾ **cup** of the mozzarella cheese and **2 tablespoons** of the Parmesan cheese. Top with the remaining mozzarella and Parmesan cheeses.

3. Bake at 350°F. for 25 minutes or until hot and the cheese melts.

Broth Simmered Rice

Makes 4 servings

START TO FINISH:
25 minutes

Prepping/Cooking:
25 minutes

Easy Substitution Tip:
Substitute Swanson®
Beef **or** Vegetable **or**
Seasoned Broths for the
Chicken Broth.

1¾ cups Swanson® Chicken Broth (Regular, Natural Goodness™
   or Certified Organic)

¾ cup **uncooked** regular long-grain white rice

1. Heat the broth in a 2-quart saucepan over medium-high heat to a boil.

2. Stir in the rice. Reduce the heat to low. Cover the saucepan and cook for 20 minutes or until the rice is tender and most of the liquid is absorbed.

Fake 'Em Out Ravioli Lasagna

Makes 6 servings

Vegetable cooking spray

1 jar (27 ounces) Prego® Italian Sausage & Garlic Italian Sauce

½ cup water

1 package (30 ounces) frozen regular size cheese-filled ravioli (about 30 to 34)

1½ cups shredded mozzarella cheese (6 ounces)

Grated Parmesan cheese and chopped fresh parsley for garnish

START TO FINISH:
1 hour, 5 minutes

Prepping: 10 minutes
Baking: 45 minutes
Standing: 10 minutes

1. Heat the oven to 375°F. Spray a 13×9×2-inch baking dish with the cooking spray.

2. Stir the Italian sauce and water in a large bowl. Spread **1 cup** of the sauce in the prepared dish. Top with ½ of the ravioli, ¾ **cup** of the mozzarella cheese and **1 cup** of the sauce. Top with the remaining ravioli and sauce. Cover the dish with foil.

3. Bake for 35 minutes or until hot.

4. Uncover the dish and top with the remaining mozzarella cheese. Bake for 10 minutes more or until hot and bubbly. Let the lasagna stand for 10 minutes before serving. Garnish with the Parmesan cheese and parsley.

Oven Baked Risotto

Makes 6 servings

START TO FINISH:
55 minutes

Prepping: 10 minutes
Baking: 40 minutes
Standing: 5 minutes

1 can (10¾ ounces) Campbell's® Condensed Cream of
  Mushroom with Roasted Garlic Soup

1½ cups water

1 cup milk

¼ cup grated Parmesan cheese

2 tablespoons chopped, oil-packed sun-dried tomatoes

1 cup **uncooked** Arborio **or** converted long grain white rice

2 tablespoons chopped fresh parsley

1. Stir the soup, water, milk, cheese, tomatoes and rice in a 12×8×2-inch shallow baking dish. Cover the dish with foil.

2. Bake at 400°F. for 30 minutes.

3. Uncover the and stir. Bake for 10 minutes more or until the rice is tender and most of the liquid is absorbed. Let the risotto stand for 5 minutes before serving. Sprinkle with parsley.

Penne with Creamy Vodka Sauce

Makes 4 servings

2 jars (1 pound 10 ounces **each**) Prego® Chunky Tomato, Onion & Garlic Italian Sauce

¼ cup vodka

⅓ cup chopped fresh basil leaves

¼ teaspoon crushed red pepper

½ cup heavy cream

1 package (16 ounces) medium tube-shaped pasta (penne), cooked and drained

Grated Parmesan cheese

START TO FINISH: 25 minutes

Prepping: 5 minutes
Cooking: 20 minutes

1. Heat the Italian sauce, vodka, basil and pepper in a 3-quart saucepan over medium heat. Heat to a boil. Remove from the heat and stir in the cream.

2. Put the pasta in a large serving bowl. Pour the sauce mixture over the pasta. Toss to coat. Serve with the cheese.

Pasta and Rice

Pasta Primavera

Makes 4 servings

START TO FINISH:
25 minutes

Prepping/Cooking:
25 minutes

3 cups **uncooked** corkscrew-shaped pasta

1 bag (16 ounces) frozen vegetable combination (broccoli, cauliflower, carrots)

1 jar (1 pound 10 ounces) Prego® Traditional Italian Sauce

Grated Parmesan cheese

1. Prepare the pasta according to the package directions. Add the vegetables during the last 5 minutes of the cooking time. Drain the pasta and vegetables well in a colander.

2. Heat the Italian sauce in the same saucepot over medium heat. Add the pasta and vegetables and toss to coat with the sauce. Top with the cheese.

Wild Mushroom Rice Pilaf

Makes 8 servings

1 tablespoon olive oil

1 pound assorted wild mushrooms (portobello, shiitake, oyster **and/or** cremini), coarsely chopped

2 medium shallots, finely chopped

2 cloves garlic, minced

1 teaspoon dried thyme leaves, crushed

3½ cups Swanson® Beef Broth (Regular, Lower Sodium **or** Certified Organic)

½ cup **uncooked** wild rice

1 cup **uncooked** regular long-grain white rice

2 tablespoons chopped fresh parsley

START TO FINISH:
1 hour, 5 minutes

Prepping: 15 minutes
Cooking: 50 minutes

1. Heat the oil in a 12-inch nonstick skillet over medium heat. Add the mushrooms, shallots, garlic and thyme and cook until the vegetables are tender.

2. Stir the broth and wild rice into the skillet. Heat to a boil. Reduce the heat to low. Cover and cook for 25 minutes.

3. Stir in the white rice. Cover and cook for 20 minutes more or until the rice is tender and most of the liquid is absorbed. Stir in the parsley.

Polenta with Mushroom Bolognese

Makes 8 servings

START TO FINISH:
1 hour, 55 minutes

Prepping: 20 minutes
Cooking: 55 minutes
Cooling: 10 minutes
Baking: 30 minutes

Make Ahead Tip:

Can be prepared and assembled completely 1 day ahead. Cover the dish with plastic wrap and refrigerate at least 12 hours or overnight. Uncover the dish. Bake at 350°F. for 35 minutes or until hot.

2 tablespoons olive oil
1 large onion, chopped (about 1 cup)
2 stalks celery, chopped (about 1 cup)
2 medium carrots, chopped (about ⅔ cup)
½ teaspoon ground black pepper
1 pound assorted wild (portobello, shiitake, oyster **or** cremini mushrooms) **and/or** white mushrooms, chopped (about 8 cups)
2 medium tomatoes, chopped (about 2 cups)
2 cloves garlic, minced
2 teaspoons dried thyme leaves, crushed
1¾ cups Swanson® Beef Broth (Regular, Lower Sodium **or** Certified Organic)
6 cups water
1 pound instant polenta
½ cup grated Parmesan cheese

1. Heat the oil in a 12-inch skillet over medium heat. Add the onion, celery, carrots and black pepper and cook until the vegetables are tender.

2. Add the mushrooms, tomatoes, garlic and thyme. Cook and stir for 5 minutes.

3. Stir the broth into the skillet. Heat to a boil. Reduce the heat to low. Cover and cook for 35 minutes until the sauce is slightly thickened.

4. Heat the water in a 3-quart saucepan over high heat to a boil. Gradually add the polenta, stirring constantly. Cook for about 5 minutes or until the mixture is very thick. Remove from the heat. Stir in ¼ **cup** of the cheese. Pour into 3-quart shallow baking dish. Let cool for 10 minutes.

5. Spread the vegetable mixture over the polenta. Sprinkle with the remaining cheese.

6. Bake at 350°F. for 30 minutes or until hot.

Pasta Shapes – Pasta Sauce
Match-up

Sauce Style	Pasta Shapes
Thick Sauces *such as*	**Smooth, Sleek and Long:**
Prego® Three Cheese, Mushroom Parmesan and Ricotta Parmesan Italian Sauces	Fettuccine Fusilli Linguini Noodles Paparedelle Penne, Mostaccioli Spaghetti Vermicelli 
Thin Sauces *such as*	**Twisted, curled, ridged and stuffed:**
Prego® Marinara or Tomato Basil & Garlic Italian Sauce	Capellini (Angel Hair) Cavatappi (Corkscrew) Gemelli Orzo Penne Rigate Radiatore (Ruffled) Ravioli Rigatoni Tortellini Rotini (Spiral, Twirls) Wagon Wheels 
Chunky Sauces *such as*	**Cupped, hollowed and nestled:**
Prego® Chunky Garden, Tomato, Onion and Garlic or Hearty Meat Meatball Parmesan	Capeletti Cavatelli Conchiglie (Shells) Elbows Farfelle (Bow Ties) Gnocchi Orecchiette Ziti 

Sides and Vegetables

START TO FINISH:
40 minutes

Prepping: 10 minutes
Baking: 30 minutes

Campbell's Kitchen Tip:
You can also make this classic side dish with fresh or canned green beans. You will need either 1½ pounds fresh green beans, cut into 1-inch pieces, cooked and drained or 2 cans (about 16 ounces each) cut green beans, drained for the frozen green beans.

Green Bean Casserole

Makes 6 servings

1 can (10¾ ounces) Campbell's® Condensed Cream of Mushroom Soup (Regular **or** 98% Fat Free)

½ cup milk

1 teaspoon soy sauce

Dash ground black pepper

2 packages (10 ounces **each**) frozen cut green beans, cooked and drained

1 can (2.8 ounces) French fried onions (1⅓ cups)

1. Stir the soup, milk, soy, black pepper, green beans and ⅔ **cup** onions in a 1½-quart casserole.

2. Bake at 350°F. for 25 minutes or until hot. Stir the green bean mixture.

3. Sprinkle the remaining onions over the green bean mixture. Bake for 5 minutes more or until onions are golden brown.

Creamy Vegetables in Pastry Shells

Makes 6 servings

START TO FINISH:
35 minutes

Prepping: 30 minutes
Cooking: 5 minutes

1 package (10 ounces) Pepperidge Farm® Frozen Puff Pastry Shells

1 can (10¾ ounces) Campbell's® Condensed Cream of Mushroom Soup (Regular **or** 98% Fat Free)

⅓ cup milk **or** water

1 bag (16 ounces) frozen vegetable combination (broccoli, cauliflower, carrots), cooked and drained

1. Bake and cool the pastry shells according to package directions.

2. Stir the soup and milk in a 2-quart saucepan over medium heat. Cook and stir until the mixture is hot and bubbling.

3. Spoon the vegetables with a slotted spoon and divide among the pastry shells. Spoon the soup mixture over the vegetables and pastry shells.

Cauliflower Gratin

Makes 6 servings

1 can (10¾ ounces) Campbell's® Condensed Cream of Mushroom Soup (Regular **or** 98% Fat Free)

½ cup milk

1 clove garlic, minced

1 bag (20 ounces) frozen cauliflower flowerets, thawed (about 5 cups)

1 cup finely grated Swiss cheese (4 ounces)

¼ cup cooked crumbled bacon **or** real bacon bits

START TO FINISH: 1 hour

Prepping: 10 minutes
Baking: 50 minutes

1. Spray a 2-quart casserole with cooking spray. Stir the soup, milk, garlic, cauliflower and ½ **cup** of the cheese in the casserole. Sprinkle with the bacon and remaining cheese.

2. Bake at 350°F. for 50 minutes or until the cauliflower is tender and mixture is hot and bubbly.

Onion Varieties

Most popular cooking ingredient in America? It could be onions—they're absolutely everywhere. There are three general types: yellow, red and white. Yellow onions are generally sweetest and can be used in just about any recipe calling for onions; white onions, similar in looks to yellow, are slightly more pungent. Red or Italian onions are milder than yellow and white and are a good choice when you want to use raw onions in salads, although they're also great grilled. Popular varieties are:

Bermuda: A mild, yellow or white onion.

Leeks: These look like overgrown scallions (see below) without the bulb. Leeks are related both to the onion and garlic, but with a subtle flavor. They can be cooked as a vegetable side dish, or chopped and used in soups, stuffings and many other dishes.

Maui: Named for its home in Hawaii, this onion is juicy, with a mild flavor and a somewhat flattened shape.

Pearl Onion: The size of a marble, pearl onions are white onions with a mild flavor. They're usually served cooked with cream or they're pickled and used as a condiment (or in a cocktail).

Scallions: Also called Green Onions or Spring Onions. Scallions are essentially

immature onions, with a small bulb and a straight, dark green stem. Both the bulb and stem are used, although some recipes will indicate a preference for one or the other.

Shallots: They may look like heads of garlic without the papery skins, but shallots really are a member of the onion family and they have the onion taste to prove it. Shallots can be used similarly to onions, but they're especially popular for sauces and gravies and any other dish that needs only a very mild onion taste.

Spanish Onion: A yellow-skinned onion that's more spherical than a regular onion.

Texas Sweet: Also called Texas Spring Sweets. The first onion to come to market in the spring, Texas Sweets are a sweet yellow onion, similar to the Bermuda, juicy with a thin skin. The Texas Sweet has low levels of pyruvate, the chemical that causes some people to tear up and cry when chopping onions.

Vidalia: Another one of the so-called "juicy" onions, Vidalia is pale yellow, very sweet, and named for the area where it's grown in Georgia.

Walla Walla: Named for its birthplace, these onions are large, juicy and golden but generally not available outside Washington State except by mail order.

Mexican Corn Casserole

Makes 6 servings

Vegetable cooking spray

1 can (10¾ ounces) Campbell's® Condensed Cheddar Cheese Soup

1 cup Pace® Chunky Salsa

1 bag (16 ounces) frozen whole kernel corn, thawed (about 4 cups)

1 cup coarsely crushed tortilla chips

START TO FINISH: 35 minutes

Prepping: 5 minutes
Baking: 30 minutes

1. Spray a 2-quart casserole with the cooking spray. Stir the soup, salsa and corn into the prepared dish. Sprinkle the tortilla chips over the corn mixture.

2. Bake at 350°F. oven for 30 minutes or until hot and bubbly. Serve immediately.

Sides and Vegetables

Ultra Creamy Mashed Potatoes

Makes about 6 servings

START TO FINISH:
25 minutes

Prepping: 5 minutes
Cooking: 20 minutes

3½ cups Swanson® Chicken Broth (Regular, Natural Goodness™ or Certified Organic)

5 large potatoes, cut into 1-inch pieces (about 7½ cups)

½ cup light cream

2 tablespoons butter

Generous dash ground black pepper

1. Heat the broth and potatoes in a 3-quart saucepan over medium-high heat to a boil.

2. Reduce the heat to medium. Cover and cook for 10 minutes or until the potatoes are tender. Drain, reserving the broth.

3. Mash the potatoes with ¼ cup broth, cream, butter and black pepper. Add additional broth, if needed, until desired consistency.

Purchasing Potatoes

Potatoes are probably one of the most popular side dishes in American cooking. There are more than 3,000 varieties, although you probably can find only five or six in your supermarket. Here are the most common types:

Russets: Also called Idahos or Burbanks. Brown-skinned, white-fleshed, their dry texture makes them perfect for baking and a good choice for mashing and French fries.

Long Whites: Also called New Whites. These oval-shaped potatoes have a thin, tan skin and tiny eyes. They're a good all-purpose potato, but they're especially good for boiling and frying.

Round Whites: Also called Eastern Potatoes. These are similar to Long Whites, but round in shape and ideal for roasting, potato salad and scalloped potatoes.

Round Reds: Good for boiling, roasting and potato salad. "New" potatoes are Round Reds that are harvested young, with tender skins.

Yellow Flesh: Also called Yukon Golds and Yellow Finns. The yellow flesh has a buttery flavor and is good for baking, mashing and roasting.

Blue and Purple: These are becoming more common in large supermarkets and at farmer's markets. The flesh can range from white to purple to dark blue. Microwave them if you want them to retain their color; they're also good for steaming and baking.

Eggplant Tomato Gratin

Makes 8 servings

Vegetable cooking spray

1 large eggplant (about 1¼ pounds), cut into ½-inch thick slices

1 can (10¾ ounces) Campbell's® Condensed Cream of Celery Soup (Regular **or** 98% Fat Free)

½ cup milk

¼ cup grated Parmesan cheese

2 large tomatoes, cut into ½-inch thick slices (about 2 cups)

1 medium onion, thinly sliced (about ½ cup)

¼ cup chopped fresh basil leaves

¼ cup Italian-seasoned dry bread crumbs

1 tablespoon chopped fresh parsley (optional)

1 tablespoon olive oil

START TO FINISH:
55 minutes

Prepping: 20 minutes
Baking: 25 minutes
Standing: 10 minutes

Make Ahead Tip:
Can be prepared ahead up to topping with the bread crumb mixture. Cover the dish with plastic wrap. Refrigerate for at least 12 hours or overnight. Uncover the dish. Sprinkle with the bread crumb mixture. Bake at 400°F. for 30 minutes or until hot and golden brown.

1. Heat the oven to 425°F. Spray a baking sheet with cooking spray. Arrange the eggplant on the sheet in a single layer. Bake for 20 minutes or until the eggplant is tender, turning halfway through baking. Spray a 13×9×2-inch shallow baking dish with cooking spray.

2. Stir the soup, milk and cheese in a small bowl. Put **half** of the eggplant, **half** of the tomatoes, **half** of the onion, **2 tablespoons** of the basil and **half** of the soup mixture in the prepared dish. Repeat the layers. Mix the bread crumbs and parsley with the oil in a small bowl. Sprinkle the bread crumb mixture over the soup mixture.

3. Reduce the oven temperature to 400°F. Bake for 25 minutes more or until hot and topping is golden brown. Let the gratin stand for 10 minutes before serving.

Creamy Baked Carrots

Makes 6 servings

START TO FINISH:
45 minutes

Prepping: 5 minutes
Baking: 40 minutes

Vegetable cooking spray

1 can (10¾ ounces) can Campbell's® Condensed Cream of Celery Soup (Regular **or** 98% Fat Free)

½ cup milk

½ teaspoon dried thyme leaves, crushed

1 bag (20 ounces) frozen crinkle-cut carrots, thawed (about 5 cups)

1 can (2.8 ounces) French fried onions (1⅓ cups)

1. Spray a 2-quart casserole with cooking spray. Stir the soup, milk, thyme, carrots and ⅔ **cup** of the onions in the prepared dish.

2. Bake at 350°F. for 35 minutes. Stir the carrot mixture.

3. Sprinkle the remaining onions over the carrot mixture. Bake for 5 minutes more or until carrots are tender and onions are golden brown.

Potato Kabobs with Cheese Sauce

Makes 6 servings

  6 medium baking potatoes (about 2 pounds)
  2 tablespoons vegetable oil
  1 can (10¾ ounces) Campbell's® Condensed Cheddar
     Cheese Soup
 ⅓ cup milk

START TO FINISH:
35 minutes

Prepping: 5 minutes
Grilling: 30 minutes

1. Cut the potatoes in half lengthwise. Cut each half crosswise into 4 pieces. Thread the potatoes on **6** skewers. Brush with the oil.

2. Lightly oil a grill rack and heat the grill to medium-high. Grill the kabobs for 30 minutes or until the potatoes are tender, turning halfway through cooking.

3. Heat the soup and milk in a 2-quart saucepan over medium-high heat until it's hot. Spoon the soup mixture over the potatoes.

Creamy Corn Pudding

Makes 6 servings

     Butter
  1 can (10¾ ounces) Campbell's® Condensed Cream of Chicken
     Soup (Regular **or** 98% Fat Free)
 ½ cup milk
  2 eggs
  1 can (16 ounces) whole kernel corn, drained
 ½ cup cornmeal
 ¼ cup grated Parmesan cheese
  1 tablespoon chopped fresh chives

START TO FINISH:
45 minutes

Prepping: 10 minutes
Baking: 35 minutes

Sides and Vegetables

1. Heat the oven to 350°F. Butter a 1½-quart casserole.

2. Beat the soup, milk and eggs in a medium bowl with a whisk. Stir in the corn, cornmeal, cheese and chives. Pour the soup mixture in the prepared casserole.

3. Bake for 35 minutes or until puffed and golden brown.

Broccoli 'n' Cheese Casserole

Makes 6 servings

START TO FINISH:
35 minutes

Prepping: 5 minutes
Baking: 30 minutes

Vegetable cooking spray

1 can (10¾ ounces) Campbell's® Condensed Cream of Mushroom Soup (Regular **or** 98% Fat Free)

½ cup milk

1 tablespoon Dijon-style mustard

1 bag (16 ounces) frozen broccoli flowerets, thawed (about 4 cups) **or** your favorite vegetable

1 cup shredded Cheddar cheese (4 ounces)

1 cup Italian-seasoned dry bread crumbs

2 tablespoons butter, melted

1. Spray a 2-quart casserole with cooking spray. Stir the soup, milk, mustard, broccoli and cheese in the prepared dish.

2. Mix the bread crumbs and butter in a small bowl and sprinkle over the broccoli mixture.

3. Bake at 350°F. for 30 minutes or until mixture is hot and bubbly.

Simmered Vegetables

Makes 4 servings

START TO FINISH:
20 minutes

Prepping: 5 minutes
Cooking: 15 minutes

1 can (10½ ounces) Campbell's® Condensed Chicken Broth

½ cup water

4 cups cut up fresh **or** 1 bag (20 ounces) frozen vegetable combination (broccoli, cauliflower, carrots)

Heat the broth, water and vegetables in a 2-quart saucepan over medium-high heat to a boil. Reduce the heat to low. Cover and cook for 5 minutes or until the vegetables are tender. Drain.

Moist & Savory Stuffing

Makes 4 cups

1¾ cups Swanson® Chicken Broth (Regular, Natural Goodness™ or Certified Organic)

Generous dash ground black pepper

1 stalk celery, coarsely chopped (about ½ cup)

1 small onion, coarsely chopped (about ¼ cup)

4 cups Pepperidge Farm® Herb Seasoned Stuffing

START TO FINISH:
15 minutes

Prepping: 5 minutes
Cooking: 10 minutes

1. Heat the broth, black pepper, celery and onion in a 2-quart saucepan over high heat to a boil. Reduce the heat to low. Cover and cook for 5 minutes or until the vegetables are tender.

2. Add the stuffing and stir lightly to coat.

Layered Cranberry Walnut Stuffing

Makes 6 servings

START TO FINISH:
35 minutes

Prepping: 10 minutes
Baking: 25 minutes

2 boxes (6 ounces **each**) Pepperidge Farm® Stuffing Mix
1½ cups Swanson® Chicken Broth (Regular, Natural Goodness™ or Certified Organic)
2 tablespoons butter
1 can (16 ounces) whole cranberry sauce
½ cup walnuts, toasted and chopped

1. Prepare the stuffing using the broth and butter according to the package directions.

2. Spoon **half** of the stuffing into a 2-quart casserole. Spoon **half** of the cranberry sauce over the stuffing. Sprinkle with ¼ **cup** of the walnuts. Repeat the layers.

3. Bake at 350°F. for 25 minutes or until hot.

Harvest Stuffing

Makes 8 servings

- **1 tablespoon olive oil**
- **1 large onion, chopped (about 1 cup)**
- **2 stalks celery, chopped (about 1 cup)**
- **1 medium apple, cored and diced (about 1 cup)**
- **1¾ cups Swanson® Chicken Broth (Regular, Natural Goodness™ or Certified Organic)**
- **1 cup diced dried apricots**
- **1 cup dried cranberries**
- **2 tablespoons chopped fresh thyme or ½ teaspoon dried thyme leaves, crushed**
- **6 cups Pepperidge Farm® Cubed Country Style Stuffing**

START TO FINISH: 25 minutes

Prepping: 15 minutes
Cooking: 10 minutes

Make Ahead Tip:
Prepare as directed and let cool to room temperature. Spoon into a greased 2-quart casserole. Cover and refrigerate. Remove from refrigerator and allow to come to room temperature. Uncover the dish. Heat in a 350°F. oven for 20 minutes or until hot.

1. Heat the oil in a 12-inch skillet over medium-high heat. Add the onion, celery and apple. Cook and stir for 5 minutes or until the vegetables are tender.

2. Stir the broth, apricots, cranberries and thyme into the skillet. Heat to a boil. Remove from the heat.

3. Put the stuffing in a large serving bowl. Pour the broth mixture over the stuffing. Stir lightly to coat. Serve immediately, or cover and keep warm in a 350°F. oven for up to 30 minutes.

Sides and Vegetables

Scalloped Apple Bake

Makes 6 servings

START TO FINISH:
1 hour, 5 minutes

Prepping: 25 minutes
Baking: 40 minutes

4 tablespoons butter, melted
¼ cup sugar
2 teaspoons grated orange peel
1 teaspoon ground cinnamon
1½ cups Pepperidge Farm® Corn Bread Stuffing
½ cup pecan halves, coarsely chopped
1 can (16 ounces) whole berry cranberry sauce
⅓ cup orange juice **or** water
4 large cooking apples, cored and thinly sliced (about 6 cups)

1. Stir the butter, sugar, orange peel, cinnamon, stuffing and pecans in a small bowl. Set the mixture aside.

2. Stir the cranberry sauce, juice and apples in a large bowl. Add **half** of the stuffing mixture and stir lightly to coat. Spoon into an 8-inch square baking dish. Sprinkle the remaining stuffing mixture over the apple mixture.

3. Bake at 375°F. for 40 minutes or until the apples are tender.

Sausage Corn Bread Stuffing

Vegetable cooking spray

¼ pound bulk pork sausage

1¼ cups water

1 tablespoon chopped fresh parsley **or** 1 teaspoon dried parsley flakes

½ cup whole kernel corn

½ cup shredded Cheddar cheese

4 cups Pepperidge Farm® Corn Bread Stuffing

1. Spray a 1½-quart casserole with cooking spray. Cook the sausage in a 10-inch skillet over medium-high heat until the sausage is well browned, stirring frequently to break up meat. Pour off any fat.

2. Stir the water, parsley, corn and cheese into the skillet. Add the stuffing and stir lightly to coat. Spoon the stuffing mixture into the prepared dish. Cover the dish with foil.

3. Bake at 350°F. for 25 minutes or until hot.

START TO FINISH:
45 minutes

Prepping: 20 minutes
Baking: 25 minutes

Make Ahead Tip:
This recipe may be prepared through step 2 and refrigerated immediately overnight. Remove from refrigerator and bake as in step 3.

Desserts

Chocolate Cherry Ice Cream Cake

Campbell's Kitchen Tip:
Ice cream is easier to
spread when it's slightly
softened. Let the ice
cream sit at room
temperature for about
10 minutes and spread
gently with a flexible
spatula to make an even
layer.

Makes 10 servings

- 1 package (6 ounces) Pepperidge Farm® Milano® Distinctive Cookies
- 1 container (1.75 quarts) black cherry ice cream
- 2 jars (17 ounces **each**) chocolate ice cream sauce
- 1 container (1.75 quarts) vanilla ice cream
  Sweetened whipped cream for garnish
  Frozen pitted dark cherries, thawed for garnish

1. Stand **10** cookies on their sides along the edge of a 9-inch springform pan, forming a ring. Coarsely chop the remaining cookies.

2. Spoon the black cherry ice cream into the pan and spread into an even layer. Spoon **1** jar of the chocolate sauce over the ice cream. Sprinkle with the coarsely chopped cookies. Freeze for 15 minutes.

3. Evenly spread the vanilla ice cream over the cookie layer. Pour the remaining chocolate sauce in the center, spreading into a circle to within 1-inch of the edge. Pipe the whipped cream around the top edge. Freeze for 2 hours or until firm.

4. Place cherries on top of the chocolate sauce just before serving.

Baked Pumpkin Custard Tarts

Makes 12 servings

START TO FINISH:
2 hours, 10 minutes

Prepping: 15 minutes
Baking: 1 hour,
  5 minutes
Cooling: 50 minutes

Vegetable cooking spray
½ cup sugar
1 teaspoon cornstarch
1 teaspoon ground cinnamon
¼ teaspoon ground cloves
1 can (15 ounces) pumpkin pie mix (1½ cups)
1 can (12 ounces) evaporated milk
4 eggs
2 tablespoons milk
2 packages (10 ounces **each**) Pepperidge Farm® Frozen Puff
  Pastry Shells
Sweetened whipped cream
Pumpkin pie spice for garnish

1. Heat the oven to 325°F. Spray a 9-inch pie plate with cooking spray and set aside.

2. Mix the sugar, cornstarch, cinnamon and cloves in a large bowl. Stir in the pumpkin pie mix, evaporated milk, eggs and milk into the sugar mixture. Pour the pumpkin mixture into the prepared dish.

3. Bake for 50 minutes or until a knife inserted in the center comes out clean. Cool on a wire rack.

4. Bake and cool the pastry shells according to the package directions. Spoon ⅓ **cup** pumpkin custard into each shell. Top with whipped cream and sprinkle with pumpkin pie spice.

Bourbon Orange Chocolate Lady Dessert

Makes 4 servings

2 fluid ounces (4 tablespoons) bourbon **or** orange juice

1 bag (7 ounces) Pepperidge Farm® Orange Milano® Distinctive Cookies

1 pint Godiva® Belgian Dark Chocolate Ice Cream, softened
  Orange slices
  Orange peel

START TO FINISH:
1 hour

Prepping: 15 minutes
Freezing: 45 minutes

Cooking for a Crowd:
Recipe may be doubled.

1. Heat the bourbon in a 1-quart saucepan over high heat to a boil. Reduce the heat to low. Cook for 3 minutes. Remove from heat and let cool. Crush **3** of the cookies.

2. Stir the bourbon, ice cream and crushed cookies in a small bowl.

3. Freeze for 45 minutes or until the mixture is firm. Scoop into dessert dishes. Garnish with orange slices, orange peel and remaining whole cookies, if desired.

Chocolate and Coconut Cream Fondue

Makes 3 cups

START TO FINISH:
15 minutes

Prepping: 5 minutes
Cooking: 10 minutes

Leftover Tip:

Any remaining fondue can be used as an ice cream or dessert topping. Cover and refrigerate in an airtight container. Reheat in saucepan until warm.

1 can (15 ounces) cream of coconut

1 fluid ounce (2 tablespoons) rum (optional) **or** 1 teaspoon rum extract

1 package (12 ounces) semi-sweet chocolate pieces

Suggested Dippers: Assorted Pepperidge Farm® Cookies, Pepperidge Farm® Graham Giant Goldfish® Baked Snack Crackers, whole strawberries, banana chunks, dried pineapple pieces **and/or** fresh pineapple chunks

1. Stir the cream of coconut, rum, if desired and chocolate in a 2-quart saucepan. Heat over medium heat until the chocolate melts, stirring occasionally.

2. Pour the chocolate mixture into a fondue pot or slow cooker.

3. Serve warm with the *Suggested Dippers*.

Bread and Butter Pudding

Makes 8 servings

- **1 stick butter (½ cup), softened**
- **1 loaf (16 ounces) Pepperidge Farm® Toasting White Bread**
- **2 teaspoons ground cinnamon**
- **¼ cup currants**
- **6 eggs**
- **2 egg yolks**
- **½ cup granulated sugar**
- **4 cups heavy cream**
- **2 cups milk**
- **1 teaspoon vanilla extract**
- **2 tablespoons packed brown sugar**

**START TO FINISH:
1 hour, 5 minutes**

Prepping: 10 minutes
Baking/Cooking:
  50 minutes
Standing: 5 minutes

1. Heat the oven to 350°F. Grease a 13×9×2-inch shallow baking dish with some of the butter. Spread the remaining butter on the bread slices. Cut each bread slice in half diagonally. Layer ½ of the bread slices in the prepared dish. Sprinkle with ½ of the cinnamon and ½ of the currants. Repeat with the remaining bread slices, cinnamon and currants.

2. Beat the eggs, egg yolks and granulated sugar with a whisk or fork in a large bowl. Heat the cream and milk in a 2-quart saucepan over low heat until the mixture is warm. Stir in the vanilla. Stir some of the cream mixture into the egg mixture. Return the egg mixture to the saucepan. Pour over the bread. Let stand for 5 minutes. Sprinkle with the brown sugar.

3. Bake for 40 minutes or until the custard is set. Serve warm or at room temperature.

Time-Saving Tip:
Substitute an 8-cup glass measuring cup for the saucepan. Pour the cream and milk in the cup. Microwave on MEDIUM (50% power) for about 7 minutes or until warm.

Make Ahead Tip:
Prepare the recipe through step 2 up to 1 day ahead but do not bake. Cover and refrigerate overnight. Bake at 350°F. for 40 minutes or until the custard is set.

Super Chunky Fudge

Makes 2 pounds

START TO FINISH:
2 hours, 25 minutes

Prepping: 15 minutes
Cooking: 10 minutes
Refrigerating: 2 hours

Holiday Tip:
To wrap for gift-giving, arrange each piece of fudge in a decorative paper cupcake liner. Wrap with colored plastic wrap and close with twist-tie or ribbon.

1 bag (5.1 ounces) Pepperidge Farm® Mini Chocolate Chunk Cookies, coarsely crumbled (about 2 cups)

1 cup miniature marshmallows
    Vegetable cooking spray

3 cups semi-sweet chocolate pieces (18 ounces)

1 can (14 ounces) sweetened condensed milk

⅛ teaspoon salt

1 teaspoon vanilla extract

1. Reserve ½ cup crumbled cookies and ¼ cup marshmallows. Line an 8-inch square baking pan with foil. Spray the foil with cooking spray. Heat the chocolate, milk and salt in a 2-quart saucepan over low heat until the chocolate melts, stirring often.

2. Remove the chocolate mixture from the heat and stir in remaining crumbled cookies, remaining marshmallows and vanilla. Spread the mixture evenly into the prepared pan. Press the reserved cookies and marshmallows into top of fudge.

3. Refrigerate for 2 hours or until firm. Remove fudge from pan and peel away foil. Cut into 16 squares. Wrap in foil. Store in the refrigerator.

Chocolate Mousse Napoleons

Makes 18 servings

½ **of a 17.3 ounce package Pepperidge Farm® Frozen Puff Pastry Sheets (1 sheet)**

1 **cup heavy cream**

¼ **teaspoon ground cinnamon**

1 **package (6 ounces) semi-sweet chocolate pieces (1 cup), melted and cooled**

1 **square (1 ounce) semi-sweet chocolate, melted**
   Confectioners' sugar

START TO FINISH:
1 hours, 20 minutes

Thawing: 40 minutes
Prepping: 25 minutes
Baking: 15 minutes

Easy Substitution Tip:
Substitute 2 cups thawed frozen non-dairy or dairy whipped topping for the heavy cream.

1. Thaw the pastry sheet at room temperature for 40 minutes or until it's easy to handle. Heat the oven to 400°F. Lightly grease a baking sheet.

2. Unfold the pastry sheet on a lightly floured surface. Cut into 3 strips along fold marks. Cut each strip into 6 rectangles. Place the rectangles 2 inches apart on the baking sheet.

3. Bake for 15 minutes or until golden. Remove from baking sheet and cool on wire rack.

4. Beat the cream and cinnamon in a medium bowl with an electric mixer at high speed until stiff peaks form. Fold in the melted chocolate pieces.

5. Split each pastry rectangle into 2 layers forming a total of 36 layers. Spread some chocolate filling on 18 of the bottom layers. Top with remaining 18 top layers. Serve immediately or cover and refrigerate up to 4 hours.

6. Drizzle pastries with melted chocolate and sprinkle with confectioners' sugar just before serving.

Mini Chocolate Cookie Cheesecakes

Makes 16 servings

START TO FINISH:
3 hours, 40 minutes

Prepping: 20 minutes
Baking: 20 minutes
Cooling: 1 hour
Refrigerating: 2 hours

Campbell's Kitchen Tip:
For a refreshing flavor, use the Pepperidge Farm® Mini Mint Milano® Cookies instead of the regular ones.

16 (2½-inch) foil baking cups
 2 packages (4.9 ounces **each**) Pepperidge Farm® Mini Milano® Distinctive Cookies
 2 packages (8 ounces **each**) cream cheese, softened
½ cup sugar
 2 eggs
½ teaspoon vanilla extract

1. Heat the oven to 350°F. Put the foil baking cups into 16 (2½-inch) muffin-pan cups or on a baking sheet. Place **2** cookies in the bottom of each cup and set aside. Cut the remaining cookies in half.

2. Beat the cream cheese, sugar, eggs and vanilla in a medium bowl with an electric mixer at medium speed until smooth. Spoon the cheese mixture into the baking cups filling each cup ¾ full. Insert **2** cookie halves, with the cut ends down, into the cheese mixture of each cup.

3. Bake for 20 minutes or until the centers are set. Cool the cheesecakes on a wire rack for 1 hour. Refrigerate the cheesecakes for at least 2 hours before serving.

Chocolate Triangles

Makes 32 triangles

1 package (17.3 ounces) Pepperidge Farm® Frozen Puff Pastry Sheets

2 egg yolks, beaten

2 teaspoons water

¾ cup semi-sweet chocolate pieces **or** chunks

Confectioners' sugar

START TO FINISH:
1 hour, 45 minutes

Thawing: 40 minutes
Prepping: 25 minutes
Freezing: 15 minutes
Baking: 15 minutes
Cooling: 10 minutes

1. Thaw the pastry sheets at room temperature for 40 minutes or until they're easy to handle. Heat the oven to 375°F. Beat the egg yolks and water in a cup with a fork.

2. Unfold **1** pastry sheet on a lightly floured surface. Roll the sheet into a 16-inch square. Brush the pastry lightly with some of the egg mixture. Cut the pastry sheet into 16 (4-inch) squares.

3. Put **1 teaspoon** chocolate pieces onto the center of each square. Fold the pastry over the filling to form a triangle and press the edges together to seal. Press the sealed edges with the tines of a fork. Prick the center of each triangle. Repeat with remaining pastry and chocolate pieces. Put triangles on a shallow-sided baking pan. Brush triangles with egg mixture. Freeze triangles for 15 minutes or until firm. Put triangles on 2 ungreased baking sheets.

4. Bake for 15 minutes or until the triangles are puffed and golden. Remove the triangles from the baking sheet and cool slightly on wire rack. Sprinkle triangles with confectioners' sugar. Serve warm.

Desserts

Fishy Families

Makes 1 pound

START TO FINISH:
36 minutes,
15 seconds

Prepping: 5 minutes
Cooking: 1 minute,
15 seconds
Refrigerating:
30 minutes

Holiday Tip:

To wrap for gift-giving, arrange clusters in small candy box lined with colored plastic wrap. Have children decorate the outside of the box with markers, sequins, stickers, etc.

1 package (12 ounces) semi-sweet chocolate pieces (2 cups)
2½ cups Pepperidge Farm® Pretzel Goldfish® Baked Snack Crackers
1 container (4 ounces) multi-colored nonpareils

1. Line a baking sheet with waxed paper and set it aside. Place the chocolate in a microwavable bowl. Microwave on HIGH for 1 minute. Stir. Microwave at 15 second intervals, stirring after each, until the chocolate melts. Stir in the crackers to coat.

2. Scoop up the cracker mixture with a tablespoon and drop onto the prepared baking sheet. Sprinkle with the nonpareils. Repeat with the remaining cracker mixture and nonpareils.

3. Refrigerate for 30 minutes or until the mixture is firm. Store in the refrigerator.

Quick & Easy Berry Shortcakes

Makes 12 servings

1	box (16 ounces) angel food cake mix
1¼	cups Diet V8 Splash® Berry Blend Juice
6	cups cut-up fresh strawberries, blueberries **and** raspberries
1½	cups thawed light whipped topping

START TO FINISH:
2 hours, 20 minutes

Prepping: 10 minutes
Baking: 40 minutes
Cooling: 1 hour,
 30 minutes

1. Heat the oven to 350°F. Prepare the cake mix according to the package directions, substituting juice for the water. Pour the batter into a 10-inch tube pan.

2. Bake for 40 minutes or until the crust is golden brown and cracked. Hang pan upside down on a heatproof glass bottle until completely cool, about 1½ hours.

3. Cut the cake into 24 slices. For each serving, place **1** cake slice on a serving plate, top with ¼ **cup** berries and **1 tablespoon** whipped topping, top with another cake slice, ¼ **cup** berries and **1 tablespoon** whipped topping. Repeat with remaining cake slices, berries and whipped topping.

Desserts

Sweet Potato Pie

Makes 8 servings

**START TO FINISH:
4 hours, 45 minutes**

Prepping: 15 minutes
Baking: 1 hour
Cooling: 3 hours,
30 minutes

Easy Substitution Tip:
Substitute 1¾ cups
drained and mashed
canned sweet potatoes
for fresh mashed sweet
potatoes. Beat with
cream until fluffy and
almost smooth.

3 large sweet potatoes, peeled and cut into cubes
(about 3 cups)
¼ cup heavy cream
1 can (10¾ ounces) Campbell's® Condensed Tomato Soup
1 cup packed brown sugar
3 eggs
1 teaspoon vanilla extract
½ teaspoon ground cinnamon
½ teaspoon ground nutmeg
1 (9-inch) unbaked pie crust

1. Heat the oven to 350°F. Put the potatoes in a 3-quart saucepan with
enough water to cover them. Heat the potatoes over medium-high heat
to a boil. Reduce the heat to low. Cover and cook the potatoes for
10 minutes or until they're fork-tender. Drain the potatoes well in a
colander.

2. Place the potatoes in a
large bowl. Add the cream.
Beat the potatoes with an
electric mixer at medium
speed until the potatoes are
fluffy and almost smooth.
Add the soup, brown sugar,
eggs, vanilla, cinnamon and
nutmeg. Beat at low speed
until the ingredients are
mixed. Spoon the potato
mixture into the prepared
crust and place the pie plate
on a baking sheet.

3. Bake for 1 hour or until
the center is almost set.
Cool the pie in the pan on a
wire rack to room
temperature.

Working with Puff Pastry

It's so easy to make incredibly beautiful and delicious desserts when you use puff pastry. With Pepperidge Farm®, the work has been done for you: Just unroll, thaw, cut, fill, bake—presto! You have an impressive dessert that looks like you worked with a pastry chef for days. Here are some tips for using puff pastry:

Thawing Pastry Sheets

● Remove as many pastry sheets as needed. Wrap unused sheets in plastic wrap or foil and return them to the freezer.

● To quick-thaw, separate the pastry sheets, covering each one with a piece of plastic wrap. Thaw the sheets at room temperature for about 40 minutes.

● Or thaw in the fridge: Pastry sheets placed in the refrigerator will be ready to use in about 4 hours and can be held up to 2 days. An entire package thaws in about 6 hours. (This method is preferred by chefs because the sheets will defrost more completely and evenly.)

Shaping Pastry Sheets

● Work with 1 pastry sheet at a time; keep the others in the refrigerator.

● Unfold pastry sheets on a lightly floured board, countertop or pastry cloth. If the pastry becomes too soft, chill it in the refrigerator for a few minutes.

● Handle the pastry as little as possible to ensure tenderness. Cut pastry with a sharp utensil such as a knife, pizza wheel or pastry tool. For decorative edges or shapes, use a fluted ravioli cutter or cookie cutters.

● For thin, crisp pastries, roll sheets to ¼-inch thickness.

● Seal filled pastries by brushing a mixture of beaten eggs and water between layers, then pinching or pressing them together.

● To turn pastries a deep golden-brown, brush tops with a mixture of 1 egg yolk and 1 teaspoon water just before baking. To add a special texture and flavor, sprinkle chopped nuts, seeds, ground spices or grated cheese on top.

● Many filled pastries can be refrigerated or frozen, then baked just before serving.

Baking Pastry Sheets

● Dark glazed baking sheets may bake puff pastry faster; adjust baking time if necessary.

● For extra-thin, crisp pastry, place a second baking sheet on top of the filled pastry before baking. Create a lattice pattern by topping the pastry with a metal cooling rack, then turning it at a right angle halfway through the baking.

● Bake prepared sheets in a preheated conventional oven (not a microwave). About halfway through, check progress by peeking through the oven window or opened door.

Desserts

Spiced Tomato Soup Cancakes

Makes 7 cakes

START TO FINISH:
4 hours, 20 minutes

Prepping: 20 minutes
Baking: 30 minutes
Cooling: 3 hours,
30 minutes

Holiday Tip:
To wrap for gift-giving, leave the cakes in the cans. Drizzle tops of cakes with Orange Icing. Wrap in plastic wrap. Cover cans with wrapping paper. Add pieces of ribbons, gold medallions, holiday stickers, etc.

Vegetable cooking spray
2 cups all-purpose flour
1⅓ cups sugar
2 teaspoons baking powder
1½ teaspoons ground allspice
1 teaspoon ground cinnamon
½ teaspoon **each** baking soda **and** ground cloves
1 can (10¾ ounces) Campbell's® Condensed Tomato Soup
¼ cup water
½ cup vegetable shortening
2 eggs
Orange Icing
Orange peel, chopped nuts **or** candied cherries for garnish

1. Heat the oven to 350°F. Spray **7** empty Campbell's® (10¾ ounces) soup cans with cooking spray.

2. Mix the flour, sugar, baking powder, allspice, cinnamon, baking soda and cloves in a large bowl. Add the soup, water, shortening and eggs. Beat with an electric mixer at low speed until the ingredients are mixed. Increase speed to high and beat for 4 minutes more. Spoon the batter evenly into the prepared cans and place on baking sheet.

3. Bake for 30 minutes or until a toothpick inserted in the center of the cake comes out clean. Cool in cans on wire racks. Remove the cakes from the cans.

4. Drizzle tops and sides of cakes with *Orange Icing*. Top with orange peel, nuts or cherries cut in leaf shapes for garnish.

Orange Icing: Mix **1 cup** confectioners' sugar, **2 tablespoons** orange juice and **1 teaspoon** grated orange peel.

Metric Conversion Chart

VOLUME MEASUREMENTS (dry)

1/8 teaspoon = 0.5 mL
1/4 teaspoon = 1 mL
1/2 teaspoon = 2 mL
3/4 teaspoon = 4 mL
1 teaspoon = 5 mL
1 tablespoon = 15 mL
2 tablespoons = 30 mL
1/4 cup = 60 mL
1/3 cup = 75 mL
1/2 cup = 125 mL
2/3 cup = 150 mL
3/4 cup = 175 mL
1 cup = 250 mL
2 cups = 1 pint = 500 mL
3 cups = 750 mL
4 cups = 1 quart = 1 L

VOLUME MEASUREMENTS (fluid)

1 fluid ounce (2 tablespoons) = 30 mL
4 fluid ounces (1/2 cup) = 125 mL
8 fluid ounces (1 cup) = 250 mL
12 fluid ounces (1 1/2 cups) = 375 mL
16 fluid ounces (2 cups) = 500 mL

WEIGHTS (mass)

1/2 ounce = 15 g
1 ounce = 30 g
3 ounces = 90 g
4 ounces = 120 g
8 ounces = 225 g
10 ounces = 285 g
12 ounces = 360 g
16 ounces = 1 pound = 450 g

DIMENSIONS

1/16 inch = 2 mm
1/8 inch = 3 mm
1/4 inch = 6 mm
1/2 inch = 1.5 cm
3/4 inch = 2 cm
1 inch = 2.5 cm

OVEN TEMPERATURES

250°F = 120°C
275°F = 140°C
300°F = 150°C
325°F = 160°C
350°F = 180°C
375°F = 190°C
400°F = 200°C
425°F = 220°C
450°F = 230°C

BAKING PAN AND DISH EQUIVALENTS

Utensil	Size in Inches	Size in Centimeters	Volume	Metric Volume
Baking or Cake Pan (square or rectangular)	8×8×2	20×20×5	8 cups	2 L
	9×9×2	23×23×5	10 cups	2.5 L
	13×9×2	33×23×5	12 cups	3 L
Loaf Pan	8 1/2×4 1/2×2 1/2	21×11×6	6 cups	1.5 L
	9×9×3	23×13×7	8 cups	2 L
Round Layer Cake Pan	8×1 1/2	20×4	4 cups	1 L
	9×1 1/2	23×4	5 cups	1.25 L
Pie Plate	8×1 1/2	20×4	4 cups	1 L
	9×1 1/2	23×4	5 cups	1.25 L
Baking Dish or Casserole			1 quart/4 cups	1 L
			1 1/2 quart/6 cups	1.5 L
			2 quart/8 cups	2 L
			3 quart/12 cups	3 L

Notes